THE GARDEN OF CIVRIE'S

A description of the
most Southern Point of the
FRENCH RIVIERA,
by
ADOLPHE SMITH,
Author of
"Street Life in
LONDON"
&c. &c.

I0136778

L.K
22283

Evans & Company, 14, Bridge Street, Westminster, London

PRICE HALF A CROWN, OR THREE FRANCS.

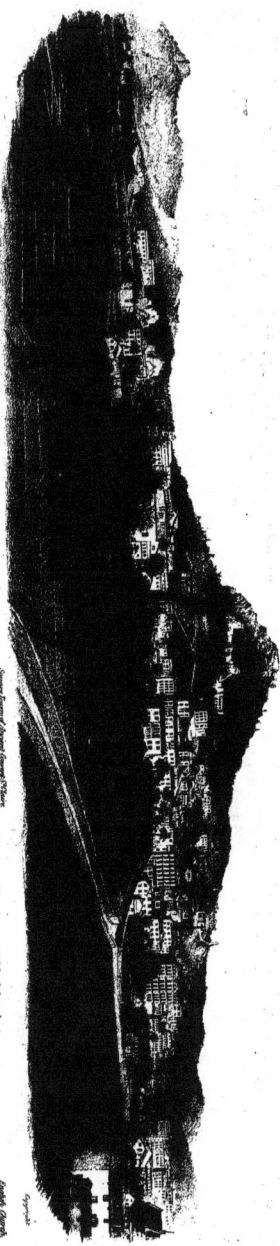

GENERAL VIEW OF HYÈRES (REPRODUCED FROM M. DEMAY'S PHOTOGRAPHES.)

THE GARDEN

OF

HYÈRES.

A DESCRIPTION OF THE MOST
SOUTHERN POINT

ON THE

FRENCH RIVIERA,

BY

ADOLPHE SMITH

(Author of "Street Life in London," &c.)

PRINTED AND PUBLISHED BY J. EVANS, AND COMPANY,
11, ᵁBRIDGE STREET, (OPPOSITE HOUSES OF PARLIAMENT,)
WESTMINSTER. LONDON, S.W,

THE GARDEN OF HYÈRES.

——:x:——

PREFACE.

Though Hyères is the oldest winter station of the Riviera, an unfortunate combination of circumstances has prevented its acquiring the same popularity as some of the more modern stations. While Cannes, Mentone, San Remo, and many other familiar towns were still unknown in the North, medical practitioners sent their patients to Hyères. It was frequented by the ancient Romans who desired to recruit their health, and has never lost its renown among those who study seriously the effect of climate in the treatment of disease.

When Lord Brougham, on his road to Naples, was accidentally detained at Cannes by the vexatious interference of the Italian police, he discovered that the Riviera possessed the climatic advantages, the magnificent vegetation and sublime scenery, he had generally sought in the South of Italy. Henceforth he wintered at Cannes, where he had the extra inducement of being nearer home, and ultimately he raised this town from a mere fishing village to the position of one of the most celebrated and certainly the most aristocratic health resorts of the Riviera. Nice, Cannes, and Monaco thus became the centres of attraction, and Hyères, which is at some distance, and not on the main line of communication, failed to share in this new development. Other places were also soon discovered close at hand, and Mentone, and San Remo acquired fame with remarkable rapidity. Dr. Henry Bennet, Dr. Arthur Hill Hassall, and Dr. Sparks, by the books they have written, rendered these two latter places inestimable service. Dr. Griffith, of Hyères, on the other hand, never cared to follow this example; and it is easy to understand that a medical practitioner should hesitate to laud the town it is to his interest invalids should frequent. As a natural result, however, Hyères, though well-known among those who are thoroughly acquainted with the resources of the Riviera, has been overtaken of late by some of the newer stations in the matter of public notoriety. In any case, there has been no work in English on Hyères, and the French books, on the subject, are now anti-dated, though I am indebted to them for many facts. The most important of these, written by M. Denis, the late Mayor of Hyères, is out of print. At best it was a ponderous and expensive volume, containing much valuable information, but compiled in a somewhat incoherent manner.

M. Amédée Aufauvre's work "Hyères et sa vallée," was a very useful and popular work, in its time, but it was published many years ago, when Hyères had no railway. The "Indicateur Topographique" is perhaps more scientific, but even this bears the date of 1861, and is a much smaller book. Putting aside the chapter in the Guide Joanne on this town, and one or two little pamphlets, there is, practically speaking, no work in French or in English, especially devoted to the description of Hyères.

Under these circumstances, I have ventured to record the result of my observations and researches made on the spot during the recent winter; and I trust the information this small volume contains will be found sufficiently useful and interesting to justify my undertaking.

ADOLPHE SMITH.

Hyères, May, 1880.

INDEX.

GARDEN of HYÈRES, Published by J. Evans & Company, 11 Bridge Street, Westminster, London. S.W.

' THE GARDEN OF HYÈRES."

CHAPTER I.

FROM LONDON TO HYÈRES.

The journey from London to Paris has been made the
subject of so many descriptions written in every tone and
every language, that we need not dwell on this portion of the
road to Hyères.   The rival routes have fortunately each some
special characteristic to recommend them to the public.   The
Calais route is the most certain, the Folkestone and Boulogne
the shortest, the Newhaven and Dieppe the prettiest.   When
other ships dare not put out to sea, the Calais mail boat,
nevertheless, braves the storm and, whatever the condition
of the tide, the harbours on either side are deep enough for
the ship to enter ; but the rail to Paris is a trifle longer, and
a little dearer. The dullness of this journey must necessarily
tempt many persons to select the Newhaven route where, not
only is the railway line shorter, but it conveys us through the
rich orchards, the gardens, the luxuriant vegetation of
Normandy. The traveller obtains a glimpse of the country
which supplies the London market with a large proportion of
the eggs, butter and poultry consumed.

From Calais to Paris, as also from Boulogne to Paris, the
journey is painfully long, and the monotony is only relieved,
for a few moments, when passing the woodland, the hills and

the valley that constitute the shooting grounds of Chantilly. Under Louis XIV, as under Napoleon III., this was the rendezvous for sportsmen and court favourites; from the great Condé to the present Duc d'Aumale, the land has been owned by members of the royal house of France. If, with the exception of this oasis, the road is uninteresting on the French side, we have, as compensation, the smiling hop fields, the cheerful villas and villages of Kent, on the English side, and the shortest possible sea passage between the two. On the other hand, the narrowest is also the worst of all seas. It imparts so peculiar and special a motion to the steamer that even old sailors, who have spent the better part of their lives on the ocean, are sometimes ill when crossing the channel. All that can be said is that the agony, though keen, is soon over. The passage should be performed in less than two hours, and rarely exceeds this time.

These facts are, however, already familiar, and in many cases painfully familiar. There is but one feature which is comparatively new with respect to the journey to Paris. From the beginning of May to the end of October, the channel may be crossed in the magnificent twin ship, the "Calais-Douvres," and, though the benefits of this innovation have been greatly exaggerated, it has undoubtedly saved many persons from sea sickness. It is a great mistake to believe the ship is free from motion. It has been my misfortune to cross the day after a gale, when the wind was still "fresh" and the sea "lumpy." There were 550 passengers crossing, and out of this number, 495 were ill. The provision of basins on board was inadequate, the confusion and suffering most painful to witness. In spite, however, of the fearful rolling the motion was an improvement on what would have been experienced in the ordinary mail boats, and as the paddle wheels are in the centre they did not come out of the water when the ship lurched to one side. The result was that the ship crossed in the usual time, and may always be relied upon on this score. The real advantage to be derived from the "Calais-Douvres" will be experienced when the sea is slight. Then delicate persons and bad sailors may cross with impunity. They would be ill in a smaller and less steady vessel even when the sea is almost calm; but in the twin-ship, the greater comfort, the freedom from overcrowding and bad ventilation combined with the absence of motion enable them to cross the dreaded channel without any objectionable consequences. Unfortunately the "Calais-Douvres" is so huge a vessel and the cost of setting her in motion so great, that it does not pay to work the ship unless there is a considerable number of travellers; hence the vessel does not run in winter. As, however, persons who are ordered to winter in the South on account of their health, should leave England before November, and not return till after the beginning of April, they will still be able to profit by this new and excellent ship.

Paris once reached, the question arises whether it is expedient to travel straight on to Hyères without halting on the road. The quickest train leaves Paris at 7.15. p.m., and reaches Hyères station at 1.26. p.m., next day. If there be any question of travelling second or third class, a slower train must be taken and the necessity of a break on the journey becomes the more imperative. In fact, if possible, a day or two of rest at Lyons and at Marseilles would render the journey far more enjoyable; only invalids travelling late in the season must be on their guard against the treacherous, dangerous climate, of damp, cold, foggy Lyons.

OUTSKIRTS OF PARIS.

From Paris to Lyons the scenery is not of a very striking description; but there are some points well worth noting. Not to mention the immediate outskirts of Paris, that recall the historic days of the great siege; *Maisons Alfort*, where the French often fought; *Villeneuve St. Georges*, one of the advance posts of the German *cordon*; the forts of Charenton and Ivry frowning on either side of the line, the train soon nears the great forest of *Fontainebleau*. There is, however, no view to be obtained of either the town or the Chateau from the railway, and though some portion of the wood may be seen, it is impossible to form any conception of this grand forest..

MONTEREAU.

After Fontainebleau, *Montereau* is soon reached. An interesting town,—for it was here on the bridge where the Seine joins the Yonne that in 1419 the Duke of Burgundy, *Jean Sans Peur*, was foully entrapped and murdered under the eyes of the Dauphin, because he patriotically offered to devote his all to driving Henry V. and the English invaders out of France.

SENS TO NUITS.

Sens, with its romantic souvenirs of Abelard and Heloise, its celebrated cathedral dating from the twelfth century, its memories of the English invasion, of Henry IV fresh from the victory of Ivry, and its feast of fools is now approached. After this we hurry past *Villeneuve sur-Yonne*, with its venerable gate and bridge; *Joigny*, with its mediæval dwellinghouses; the old Roman town of *Saint Florentin* with its high steps leading up to its church; and then the train rumbles into a larger station, the porters shout out *Tonnerre* in loud voices, and we know that the wine lands of Burgundy have been reached. *Chablis* is close at hand; *Nuits* a little further on, and these names recall the memory of good dinners, and hard fighting against the Germans.

VALLEY OF THE BRENNE.

After leaving *Montbard*, there are some pretty glimpses of scenery as the train crosses the valley of the Brenne where the chief of a hundred valleys, Vercingetorix, fought the great Cæsar with so much heroism. In this valley is situated the old town of Alesia, at once the cradle and the tomb of ancien Gaul; for under its wall Vercingetorix surrendered himself to save the brave Celtic warriors who for so long had kept Cæsar at bay. The train passes under the height of Alesia, and on its summit M. Millet's gigantic statue to Vercingetorix, standing on the pedestal designed by Viollet-le-Duc, commands the entire battle field. There is scarcely a page in French history more interesting and more pathetic than that recalled by these mementoes.[*]

TUNNEL OF BLAISY.

The tunnel of *Blaisy*, 4100 metres in length, must now be encountered. This was one of the earliest achievements of railway engineering. It was built in 1846 to 1849, and cost £311,600 while the air shafts cost more than £400,000. The tunnel which required so much time, labour, and money to pierce is passed in five minutes, and we near the Viaduct of *Fain* bridging with a double row of arches the valley of the Ouche. Three more viaducts, *Fouchères, Bouchard*, and *Matoy* follow in due course. These are noble structures which enable the traveller to obtain fine views of the surrounding country and of *Plombières*. A long tunnel cutting through rocks with occasional glimpses of light, and several smaller viaducts to carry the train over crag and crevice, now lead us to the capital of Burgundy, *Dijon*.

DIJON.

An excellent buffet, a long pause, an interesting town, and a choice of several good hotels, all combine to tempt the traveller to halt here. This is also the station where the line for Switzerland branches off and leaves the main artery. At the buffet, the Anis de Dijon will be found in profusion, (these are the simplest and most wholesome of French sweet meats), and of course there is an extensive choice of wines. Hampers are also made up at the station for persons desiring to take

---

[*] Cæsar Commentaries Book VII. Henri Martin's History of France, and Eugène Sue's romance, Les Mystères du Peuple a Travers les Siecles.

samples of Burgundy away with them. But if such a purchase be made, duty will have to be paid on entering any town. From the line nothing worth mentioning can be seen of Dijon, but persons desiring to rest here for a day or two will find much to interest them in the ancient capital of the dukes of Burgundy. Nor is there any lack of literature to explain the architectural, archiological, and historical advantages of this city. The Museum, the collection of paintings, the magnificent tombs of the dukes of Burgundy, the historical and mediæval houses, the learned societies, the theatre, the castle, the remains of the old walls, the excellent cooking, the superabundant and good food, and the still better wines, are all so many inducements to linger on the road.

CÔTE D'OR.

A few miles beyond *Dijon*, the line enters the district of the *Côte d'Or*, and the names of the stations read as a wine list :— *Gevrey Chambertin, Clos de Vougeot, Beaune, Pommard, Volnay,* and our every day friend, the familiar *Mâcon*. It cannot be said, however, that vine yards as seen from a railway carriage, when passing these stations are particularly interesting. The beauty of the leaf cannot be distinguished at a distance, the colour is often dull, and the stumpy growth of the plant in regular lines, destroys the picturesque charm of the scene, which for cheerfulness, colour, and beauty, cannot be compared to the hop fields of Kent. Still there is some fine scenery depending not on the vine but on the hills; and this notably on leaving the station of *Chagny*. *Châlon* also occupies an admirable site, and after passing *Mâcon* gracefully poised on the banks of the Soane, there is a fine view of this river and of castellated heights to the right. The whole country is thickly dotted with cottages, and farms, and wears the aspect of great prosperity.

VILLEFRANCHE.

Villefranche is the capital of the Beaujolais wine district, and it is from this source that many of the hotels of Lyons derive their supply of *ordinaire* which the traveller may consume ad-

libitum and free from all charge. South of Lyons the wine
soon losses its delicate flavour, and assumes the coarse and
strong character which makes the ordinary wines of the South
better suited for blending purposes. On leaving this station,
a fine view of the Mont d'Or range may be obtained, which
gave rise to the exaggerated saying—

> " De Villefranche a Anse
> La plus belle lieue de France."

At last, we reach the enormous station of Vaise, a suburb of
Lyons where there is a great depot of railway rolling stock, a
workshop and a goods station. From this point to the Perrache
station, the train passes through the tunnel of Saint Ireneus,
2175 metres in length, and 92 metres (301 feet) below the
summit of the mountain.

LYONS.

We are now at Lyons, a name which Barrère declared should
no longer exist. A monument was to be raised on the smoking
ruins of the great city with the simple inscription, " Lyons
waged war against freedom, Lyons is no more." It happens,
however, that Barrère is now no more, while Lyons not only
exists, but has lived to be named by Dumas, the Vice Queen of
France. Far from waging war against liberty Lyons is, on the
contrary, renowned for its devotion to Republican principles,
and is one of the most interesting towns, politically speaking
of France. After Sédan, the population of Lyons proclaimed
the Republic before the Parisians ; and the Socialistic workmen
of Lyons have fought and died with at least as much heroism
and devotion as the most fanatical Revolutionists of Belleville
or Montmartre. They are also better read than the Paris
workmen, and can discuss with more accuracy the doctrines of
Fourrier, of Proudhon, of Louis Blanc, of Blanqui, and many
other authors. The thoughtful visitor to Lyons will therefore eschew the fashionable quarters of the town and clamber
up to La Croix Rousse or visit La Guillotière. Here he may

make acquaintance with intelligent artizans who will eloquently expound the somewhat faded doctrines of Mutualism, the more modern principles of Collectivism, and dilate on the new religion which has added the word " Solidarity " to the great Republican device " Liberty, Equality, Fraternity."

Side by side with the elements that represent the most advanced ideas of the age, will be found, also firmly impregnated at Lyons, an extraordinary number of convents and monasteries, where the most reactionary doctrines are taught, where the legends of the past are still religiously cherished and the faith in modern miracles proclaimed. The sound of the convent bell seems at every turn to reply to the rude chorus of the Carmagnole; while, holding the balance between these two extremes, the wealthy middle class manufacturers persist steadfastly in their undisturbed worship of the almighty dollar. In so large and historical a town, there must of necessity, be much to see, but the panoramic views to be obtained from La Croix Rousse and la Fourvière are the most striking. Some idea of this grand sight can be gathered from the carriage windows as the railway passes by the great city.

Invalids, however, will perhaps find it more prudent to hurry past without stopping, for the climate of Lyons is extremely trying. It is cold and foggy, and recalls all the treachery of London with far greater intensity of cold in the winter. The aspect of the streets is lacking in the gaiety and movement that are so inspiriting in Paris and Marseilles; but the theatres are exceptionally good, the cafés and restaurants luxurious, and the picture galleries possess several good specimens of the old masters Teniers, Rubens, etc. The Cathedral, St. Nizier, the public buildings, the Bourse, the Hotel de Ville, the Musée Guimet, with Felix Régamey's paintings, these, and many other sights, will be found interesting and will tempt the traveller to halt a while.

On leaving Lyons, the train crosses the Rhone by a magnificent stone and iron bridge 657 feet high, from whence the
panorama already mentioned unrolls itself; then, after passing
the Guillotière station, the forts of *Colombier* and *la Motte* may
be seen on the left and the vine clad heights of *Sainte Foy* on
the right.

VIENNE.

Vienne is the first important station, and is crowned
by Mount Salomont and the ruins of its mediaeval castle,
This Celtic town founded, according to Strabon, before Rome.
will attract the historian and the archæologist, its Cathedral
its ancient buildings, its Forum and other remains of Roman
civilization are worthy of note.

The line now nears the mountain chain of Mont-Pila and
subsequently, to the right, the chateau of Mont Lys, and the
ruins of Prieuré de Notre Dame de l'Isle are to be seen before
the Rhone is again approached. Soon we are crowded in
between the Montagne de Marcon and the river, compelled to
follow its curves and able to note the islands that dot its
course. Occasional ruins on the summit of the hills, and the
vine growing on sheltered hedges, all recall the scenery of the
Rhine, particularly as each of these castles has its history, its
legends, and its architectural peculiarities.

VALENCE.

Valence is the next cathedral town, and then we pass the
ruins of Crussol, the citadel of Montélimar. Viviers, at
a distance, stands perched high on its hill, and then we reach
Pierrelatte, the station for the celebrated Chateau de Grignan
which Madame de Sévigné has so ably described. Here, as at
La Palud, the station for la Grande Chartreuse, where the
monks have become liquor distillers, we are travelling over
ground which was formerly submerged, and formed large
marshes watered by the Rhone. The chateau of Mondragon
at some distance to the right, the precipitous hill of Mornas

with its ruined castle from whence the Protestants threw the Catholics into the Rhone, during the wars of the XVI century are now passed in succession, and we approach *Orange*, the first important town of Provence.

THE OLIVE TREES.

Already from Valence a change may be observed and, as we leave the narrow defile near Viviers, an occasional olive tree may be noted on either side of the line. But the cold northern wind imparts to this portion of Provence a particularly arid appearance. M. Charles Lenthéric in his admirable and recent work, "*La Provence Maritime*," gives an eloquent sketch of this transition :—

"The olive tree appears for the first time on the slopes dominating the village of Donzère. It is here that the North ends, and the South of France begins. On all the hill sides, the sombre but useful groups which alone suit these stony lands burnt by the sun, may be seen growing. Such as it is to-day so it was centuries ago, for this tree is almost immortal, it springs up afresh out of its own decay. The old trunk hollowed out and dried is filled with stones and earth, so that it may resist the force of the wind.   *   *   *

"As we descend towards the sea and advance along the eastern coasts, following the marvellous shores of Provence, the olive trees become more and more decorative in their general aspect. The pale line of the green grows more vivid and accentuated. The trunk is more and more massive; from a shrub it develops into a tree whose summit, however, never surpasses the superb dome of the umbrella pine. From Marseilles to Toulon, the olives are still small, sturdy though remarkably fertile; it is well known that the plain of Aix supplies the best oil of Provence. Little by little the tree seems to emancipate itself, it shakes off the bond of servitude, and here and there assumes grand proportions. After Toulon and in the admirable *plaine du Luc* it continues to grow but still maintains that uniformity of shape which imparts a special physiognomy and a slightly monotonous character to the landscapes of Upper Provence."

AVIGNON.

More castles, more ruins, more hills and rocks, meet our gaze as we travel from *Orange* to *Avignon*, passing by the picturesque ramparts of the town of the Popes. The cathedral, the tombs of the popes, the Papal palace, these and many other structures connected with early Christianity are mingled with the ruins of the Roman occupation. The home of Petrarch and of John Stuart Mill, is so familiar to English readers that it is scarcely necessary to insist on the interest indissolubly connected with this historical town. I need only remark that it is not sheltered from the mistral, and invalids had better only stop here when this, the "scourge of Provence," is not threatening.

On leaving *Avignon*, the line crosses a fertile plain planted with the short mulberry trees that serve to feed the silk worms; and then reaches the Champfleury viaduct, and afterwards runs over the Durance, by a viaduct of 2752 feet in length, which is generally considered one of the most important works of the line, as it was a matter of great difficulty to discipline the waters of the Durance. From this point, a fine view can be obtained of the Lubéron chain on the left, and the wild rock *la Montagnette* crowned by the tower of Barbentane. There now remain but three important stations before reaching Marseilles. The first is Tarascon named after the fierce dragon which Saint Martha, the sister of Mary Magdalen is supposed to have tamed, and renowned for its annual fete originally organised by King René, in 1469. On these occasions there is a great display of fancy dresses, and a lay figure of a dragon in a state of fury is dragged through the streets, to be followed by another figure of the dragon in a subdued attitude with a young girl in white standing by its side. This ceremony and the many ruins, recall [the better days of Provençal history and the trace of the achievements of Saint Remy mingle with the ruins of the earlier civilization brought by the Romans.

ARLES.

The second town is *Arles,* celebrated for its pretty women and its sausages; the latter, however, are for the most part made at Tarascon. Not only are the women beautiful, but they present three distinct types, the Roman, the Greek, and the Saracen. M. Jules Canonge in his work " Arles en France " also insists that their physical likeness is rendered the more evident by the analogy of their characters, delicate and joyful as a Greek maiden, capable of lofty thoughts, and heroic devotion as the strong women of Rome, they also possess the graceful coquetishness of the Spaniard. The *Arlésienne* loves flowers, perfumes, poetry, display, excitement, fêtes, balls and serenades. Historically there is not a more interesting town than Arles in all Provence. Here Romans, Franks, Saracens, Goths and the old Gauls have struggled for supremacy. Its Roman amphitheatre, obelisk, forum, the palace of Constantine, its ramparts, together with the more modern and Christian edifices, demonstrate how great has been the part that Arles has played in the growth of civilisation both before and after the present era.

The viaduct of Arles conducts us to *la Crau,* which is the Provençal word for stony plain, this special plain measures 200 square kilometres. It was here that Hercules met the two giants Albion and Belgion, and, having exhausted his supply of arrows, invoked Jupiter who annihilated them with a shower of stones. Such is the way in which the ancients explained the presence of the innumerable stones which modern geologists declare were brought here by the Rhone and the Durance till such time as the sea beat up a barrier, and these rivers changed their course. The rocky nature of the country, especially at Saint Chamas, and the small inland sea of Berre indicate great evolutions of nature; and then, when finally we reach the two great chains of mountains that envelop *Marseilles*, and stretching out even into the sea form the islands of Pomègue, Ratonneau and the Château d'If, where Monte Christo effected his marvellous escape, the mighty change which a few hours railway travelling has enabled us to enjoy is now fully realized. Indeed, the journey from the gloom, the cold, the damp and blackness of Lyons to the brilliant sunshine, the blue sea, the clear atmosphere of Marseilles is the most pleasant and cheering transition. It is in itself sufficient to revive the "tone" of any invalid, and no pharmacopæia could possibly devise a better moral tonic.

MARSEILLES.

Marseilles is a town that cannot be described in a chapter, much less in a paragraph. The length of its history may be judged from the fact that it was founded by the Phœnicians nine hundred years before Christ. The difference of its climate may be gathered from the fact that I have left Lyons with its fountains all frozen, and the ice several inches deep, to reach Marseilles a few hours later, and find the sun so hot that most persons were walking under umbrellas to avoid its glare and heat. With more than 300,000 inhabitants, for the most part engaged in commercial pursuits, this town also offers all the interest and movement of a great sea port. It has its old, crowded, poor, picturesque, and unwholesome quarters; but there are its new boulevarts cutting right through these ancient "rookeries," notably the rue de la République, and the rue Colbert now in course of construction. But of all thorough-fares one of the most brilliant and remarkable in all Europe, is undoubtledly the Cannebière. The rue de la République cost nearly 4,000,000*l*; but the finest hotels, the best cafés, the richest shops, the broadest causeways are to

be found in the Cannebière.   This, the principal thoroughfare
of Marseilles, ends at the old port.   The shipping can be seen
from a considerable distance, and it lends a very peculiar
aspect to the street; it, is as M. Edmond About remarks, a
door opening on to the Mediterranean and leading out to the
whole world.   The Cannebière is thoroughly characteristic.
The sea gulls that flit about at its base, the masts that lift
their graceful rigging to the blue sky, the buzz of a thousand
voices, the crowd composed of every nationality, where the
turban mixes with the silk hat, the fez fraternizes with the
wide awake, these, and a hundred other peculiarities, make up
a picture that can only be found in an important centre, such
as this port where a multiplicity of nationalities unite to share
in the greatness and prosperity of the principal station on our
high road to India.

   The sights of Marseilles are naturally numerous.   There are
the new Cathedral and the old relics, the Zoological gardens,
the grand picture galleries, with a poor collection of paintings,
the Hotel de Ville, the Stock Exchange, a number of churches,
of fountains, of monuments, fine boulevards, dirty docks, and
miserable bye-streets, soap mills and oil mills, theatres and
music halls, and even a Crystal Palace; many clubs, schools of
art, and schools of science, and a special school for the study of
the special maritime growths of the Mediterranean.   Some-
thing, in short, to attract every fancy, the means of riding any
hobby.

TOULON.

   Marseilles might become a winter resort but for the fact that
it is thoroughly exposed to the Mistral.   This fearful wind
sometimes blows with such violence that it has been known to
carry horses off their feet and in October, 1879, precipitated a
carriage, driver and horse into the docks.   Hence the necessity
of pushing on to Hyères the nearest, and at the same time
the most southerly, health resort of the Riviera.   This is, however, the last and the shortest stage of the journey.   *Toulon is*

reached in a little more than an hour by the express train, and in a little less than two hours by the slower train. Here it is necessary to change carriages and, by a branch line, Hyères is approached in about three quarters of an hour. This short journey affords occasional glimpses at the Mediterranean, especially at La *Ciotat*, at *Bandols* and *Cassis* which will produce an indelible impression on all lovers of nature. The inland scenery, the gorges of *Ollioules*, the various offshoots of the Montagne Maures are grand in their colouring, their size and shape. The huge hills that surround Toulon and protect this, the French Portsmouth, cannot be viewed without emotion when we remember that it was here Napoleon first distinguished himself; and this too by defeating the English forces. Toulon, like Marseilles, has a history that dates ten centuries before the Christian era; but it has no commerce to give it life; it depends almost exclusively on its maritime arsenal and its ships of war. A few hours will suffice to obtain a general impression of the town, its narrow streets, and the very peculiar semicircle described by the shops, and cafés that line the inner dock or port. The shipping, the arsenal, and the outer port will take much longer time to visit, but Toulon is one of the regular excursions undertaken by the inhabitants of Hyères, and need not be visited on the road. It is perhaps more to the point to dine at the very good buffet which is the pride of the railway station. The trains running to Hyères as often as not, fail to correspond with the trains stopping at Toulon, and there is consequently time enough to test the reputation this buffet has acquired. For instance, the last available train from Marseilles reaches Toulon at 6.23. p.m., and the train for Hyères does not leave till 7.16. p.m. With a little pressure and persuasion the table d'hote dinner which is served at 7.10. p.m., on the arrival of the Genoa train, can be given half an hour sooner, and there are not many stations in France where so good a meal at so moderate a rate can be obtained.*

*Four francs, wine included.

On leaving Toulon the train passes through olive plantations and to the north may be seen the *Coudon*, to the south the Colle Noire and the Paradis mountains, which will soon become the landmarks of many a pleasant expedition. Then we approach the smaller hill at the foot of which the old town of Hyères nestles safely sheltered from the Mistral. But the railway station is in an exposed plain, more than a mile from the town, and it would be well for very delicate persons not to arrive here at night. If such a rare phenomenon as a fog or mist should make its appearance it is more likely to to found hovering round the railway station than any where else in the neighbourhood. The invalid should not therefore loiter on this spot but hasten to the waiting room, or be careful to shut the omnibus windows if the weather appears at all unfavourable. A great improvement will be found on reaching the higher, and more sheltered ground where the town itself is built; and then this long journey will be over. To the thoughtful the time will have passed quickly, and the fatigues of the route are easily forgotten in the magnificence of the scenery and the historical interest associated with so many stations.

HYERES; ITS CLIMATE: ITS MEDICAL AND SANITARY ASPECT.

CHAPTER II.

Though as a pleasure resort the town and neighbourhood of Hyères offer many inducements to the healthy, they are, at present, principally known for the wonderful effects of the climate on persons suffering from weak chests and lung disease. The future will prove that Hyères possesses the natural attractions necessary for a general holiday town; and art and enterprise, united with capital, will ultimately supply all the artificial means of enjoyment which may still be wanting. For the present, however, invalid, or at least delicate, persons and their friends constitute the majority of visitors, both English and French. Nor has full justice been rendered to Hyères even in this respect. Other towns on the Riviera have found able and special pleaders who have put before the British public all, and perhaps more than could fairly be said in their favour. Even the medical authors who have *Books about* given some account of all the towns on the Riviera *the Riviera.* are for the most part scarcely at pains to conceal the strong bias they feel in favour of the town where they live and practice. The one invariably reverts to Mentone, the other to San Remo, and perhaps a third will not hear a whisper against Cannes; but the force of these arguments is considerably mitigated when it is found, on inquiry, that the authors of these books own considerable property or enjoy extensive practice in the very towns which they are at such pains to extol. At Hyères, on the contrary, the English medical men have shown the good taste to remain silent, and if the town has been guilty of hiding its light under a bushel its English practitioners have not sought to increase its popularity and improve their position by writing pseudo-medical works against the neighbouring health resorts.

Fortunately, we have in Dr. C. T. Williams' book, "The Climate of the South of France," * a work where the deepest scientific knowledge and research are happily associated with the strictest impartiality. It is hardly necessary to insist, when mentioning a name nearly as familiar to the general public as to the profession at large, on the renown acquired by both Dr. C. J. B. Williams and his son, Dr. C. T. Williams, for their successful treatment of chest diseases. Their treatises on Pulmonary Consumption, on Climate in Disease, and on the Climate of the South of France, will remain the standard medical works which both the profession and the public will consult in preference. Needless to add that Dr. Williams has visited and carefully investigated the condition of all the important winter stations in the South, but resides and practices in London.

Speaking of Hyères, Dr. Williams first insists on the important fact that it is at once the nearest and yet the most southerly of all the French winter resorts. It occupies latitude 43·7° N., and is well situated in the fertile valley that runs from the sea in a north-westerly direction to the foot of the high and rugged mountains that surround the town and harbour of Toulon. On either side of the valley the Montagne du Paradis and Montagne des Oiseaux to the S.W., and the Maurettes with the Maures mountains behind to the N.E., *Topographical position of Hyères.* shelter this choice spot. Even to the S.E. the force of the sea winds is partially broken by the lofty Golden Islands that stand out at but a little distance from the coasts. Warm as Toulon is generally considered to be, Dr. Edwin Lee remarks that a great difference of temperature

---

* Longmans, Green & Co., London, 1869.

is experienced on approaching Hyères. The valley, in consequence of its sheltered position, is covered with the most luxuriant vegetation; and in support of this assertion Dr. Williams quotes some notes taken at Cannes in 1865 and at Hyères in 1866 by the Rev. D. C. Timins, giving a list of eighteen different flowers that bloomed earlier at Hyères than at Cannes. In one instance, the *Erica Arborea* bloomed thirty four days sooner at Hyères. In six cases the difference was more than twenty days, in eight cases more than ten days, in the four remaining cases the difference was under ten days. A similar *Precocity of vegetation.* table is given relating to fifty-two varieties of Lepidoptera, whose appearance takes place at the same time as the plants. In this, as with respect to the vegetation, the difference between Cannes and Hyères is equally remarkable. But at the same time it is only fair to observe that the season of 1865, when the observations were taken at Cannes, was, on the whole colder than that of 1866; the mean difference amounting in February to as much as 4° Fahr. Yet Dr. Williams remarks that this difference was not sufficient to account for the striking contrast presented by Mr Timins' table, more *Warmth.* especially as the mean temperature in April, 1865, was decidedly in favour of Cannes; it was actually 6° higher than in 1866, when the observations were made at Hyères. *

---

* Dr. Williams also quotes the following observations given to him by a lady who passed the winter of 1866-7 at Hyères. They were made twice a day in an *unoccupied* room facing the south, and where no fire whatsoever was lit :—

1867.		9 a.m.	9 p.m	1867.		9 a.m.	9 p.m.
February	20	62	61	March	4	57	56
,,	21	61	60	,,	5	57	57
,,	22	61	—	,,	6	56	56
,,	23	62	61	,,	7	56	57
,,	24	62	62	,,	8	57	58
,,	25	64	62	,,	9	58	58
,,	26	64	62	,,	10	60	64
,,	27	64	63	,,	11	62	62
,,	28	64	63	,,	12	62	64
March	2	58	57	,,	13	62	61
,,	3	57	56				

With respect to the town of Hyères, the east end is fairly sheltered from the mistral, the cold north-west wind, by the Castle Hill. The west end has no such immediate protection, but the force of the mistral is broken by the Toulon mountains, the Coudon, &c. It is important to note, however, that the mistral, before reaching Hyères, passes over a certain amount of *Wind.* sea, and is therefore not quite so dry, though it will often produce a difference of 10° Fahr. between the wet and dry bulb. Nor is the mistral, when it blews gently, an unpleasant wind; and when it blows violently, though it must confine invalids to their rooms, it is a great benefit to the country at large, for it purifies every nook and corner, and blows away the danger of epidemic diseases. Further, the sky is never so blue, or the sun so bright, the air so clear, and the weather so fine as when the mistral is blowing. To the healthy, or to these who are not suffering from lung disease and require bracing, the mistral is an invigorating wind. When the mistral has fairly set in, the invalid must make up his mind to remain indoors for one or twe days, but he may derive some consolation from the thought that the health of the friends who accompany him will benefit by the change, and that they will enjoy the fine weather. Nor is it possible in any way to entirely avoid the mistral; the whole of the Riviera at times feels the effects of its cold gusts; but its force is modified, though only modified, by the hills or mountain ranges that protects the various winter stations, and as " enjoying the advantages of this situation in a more than ordinary degree" Dr. More Madden signalizes the town of Hyères. *

At the same time, it is important to remark that Hyères is not so dry as Cannes and Nice, and, in fact, the Riviera generally. The marvellous vegetation of the plain, which is one vast garden, the trees that cover the mountains to their

* Dr. More Madden's "The Principal Health Resorts of Europe and Africa," 1876.

very summit, all contribute to increase the moisture of   *Dryness.* the air; while at the other stations the barren limestone rocks are almost devoid of any greenery. Thus it will be found that the difference between the wet and the dry bulbs is generally a degree and a half Fahr. less at Hyères than at the other stations of the Riviera; yet, as the mean difference generally amounts to 5° at Hyères, the climate may be considered very dry, but not so excessively dry as to prove injurious. The mean winter temperature, according to Dr. Williams' book published in 1869, is 47·3° Fahr.; and the average rainfall 27 inches, that is a little more than at Nice. The number of rainy days, according to M. de Valcourt, is sixty-three, or less than at Nice or Mentone. Nor is Hyères exposed to the wind known as the "vent de Nice," which, blowing straight down from the snow-clad peaks of the Alps, is nearly as objectionable as the mistral. Good temperature observations, with modern instruments, have been carried on at Hyères for many years. I have had occasion to look over the observations by Dr. Griffith, dating more than twenty years back, and fully quoted by Dr Williams, though ignored by the pseudo-scientific medical writers on the Riviera. Dr. Vidal, the corresponding member of the Central Meteorological Bureau of France, gives me the following official report of the rainfall at the   *Rainfall.* Salins des Pesquiers, which, though four miles from Hyères, corresponds within a fraction, to the rainfall in the town itself, and that observed at the Old Salins:—

	1860	61	62	63	64	65	66	67	68	69	70	71	72	73	74	75	76	77	78	79
Jan.	185	30	70	185	,,	15	32	76	15	22	78	80	145	35	45	,,	133	38	20	108
Feb.	12	160	5	,,	113	,,	,,	63	10	20	210	,,	57	55	108	12	20	,,	,,	30
March	,,	,,	55	83	103	105	70	60	15	58	,,	50	135	45	15	15	45	22	10	85
April	60	,,	,,	,,	,,	,,	17	,,	,,	40	,,	,,	48	81	124	55	53	14	40	91
May	75	50	35	62	,,	,,	27	,,	20	12	,,	48	12	24	24	18	25	8	31	120
June	38	,,	6	,,	35	,,	12	5	,,	,,	95	16	,,	20	10	52	,,	,,	72	,,
July	,,	,,	,,	,,	,,	10	,,	5	22	6	,,	,,	36	,,	10	,,	5	,,	,,	5
Aug.	8	,,	12	,,	,,	24	10	15	95	7	135	,,	5	40	,,	,,	50	30	285	,,
Sept.	66	,,	165	30	,,	,,	43	,,	160	30	,,	60	12	20	155	22	,,	,,	5	55
Oct.	,,	67	130	90	160	25	47	97	175	,,	,,	15	300	133	100	58	90	33	37	47
Nov.	92	20	300	35	157	112	22	35	60	130	128	253	54	170	16	,,	71	30	168	36
Dec.	172	,,	100	10	170	53	20	15	,,	30	220	50	155	,,	70	115	30	15	115	13
	628	827	878	495	738	344	309	374	572	355	966	572	953	623	677	347	522	190	783	1591

The average for the above twenty years is 555 millimeters. This calculation was made before the rainfall of the last two months of 1879 was made known. This is equivalent to a rainfall of 20·80 inches, and is therefore considerably below Dr. Williams' estimate, which, however, was taken at an anterior period. During the months of October, November, December, 1879, of January, February, March, and April, 1880, there fell 239·9 millimeters of rain; that is, 9·43 inches according to the official report. Perhaps, however, the following synopsis of the meteorological observations taken during the worst of all years on modern record will suffice for the present purpose.

Days of sunshine. The instruments were placed in a Stevenson's screen, and kept in the most exposed part of the garden behind the Hotel des Iles d'Or, and consequently represent temperatures to which no invalid would ever be subjected:—

SYNOPSIS OF METEOROLOGICAL OBSERVATIONS TAKEN AT HYERES, 1879—80.

Month.	Days of sunshine	Days of wind	Days on which rain fell	Rainfall inches.	Average Temperature Max.	Min.
1879. October (from 15th)	13	3	4	—	—	—
November	23	3	7	1·50	59·52	43·33
December	28	3	1	·50	51·92	33·06
1880. January	25	5	4	·58	54·63	37
February	22	2	7	1·54	59·25	41 99
March	25	2	8	·92 (?)	62·57	44·72

Every one will remember that during the above winter the Seine, the Rhine, and a number of other rivers were frozen over, that the cold at Paris and in England was excessive and exceptional; the severity of the weather, in fact, was so intense that it assumed the proportions of a public disaster. Yet at Hyères it barely froze for an hour or two, and it was almost always possible to go out in the warm sunshine for several hours each day.

Apart from general climatic advantages common to the French and Italian Riviera, Hyères possesses special *Protection* qualifications which are most important from the *from irritating sea* medical point of view. Most of the other stations *breezes.* may be compared to a Dutch oven. In front, there is the broiling sun, and the sea reflects its rays and glare. Immediately behind, leaving barely room for the building of the town, the high limestone mountains throw back the heat and constitute what may be compared to the oven. The openness of the Hyères valley, with the consequent free circulation of the air, is naturally considered one of its great advantages. The sea is a good three miles away, and thus we not only escape the sea-breeze which blows along the Mediterranean coast from 10 a.m. to 3 or 4 p.m., on sunny days and can scarcely reach so far inland, but all the injurious effects which undoubtedly result from the neighbourhood of the sea are avoided. . It must be borne in mind that the tide of the Mediterranean is hardly perceptible; that whereas the saline residue of a 100 part of Atlantic water, taken off Bayonne, amounts, according to Messrs Bouillon, Lagrange de Vogel's Analysis, to 3·80, that of the Mediterranean water, taken off Marseilles, amounted to 4·10. This renders the sea air more than usually exciting; and this is notoriously injurious in many, if not in the majority, of cases of lung disease, and especially in bronchial affections. This class of patient suffers from the exaggerated dryness and the saline breezes that afflict most of the stations on the Riviera.

The broad stretch of vegetation lying between the town of Hyères and the sea, the massive rocks and hills of the islands that are so near the coast, all tend to protect the town from the exciting salt sea-breezes, and this circumstance, taken in combination with the slight moisture which softens the air, produces a sedative effect. Many persons of *Sedative effect of the* excitable dispositions who are unable to sleep at *climate.* most of the stations on the Riviera enjoy good rest when once they reach Hyères. Hence Dr Williams, in harmony with innumerable other medical authorities, is led to conclude that "the climate of Hyères is the least exciting and the least stimulating of all health-resorts of this region. In fact, it sometimes has a sedative effect." Therefore, it is urged that all phthisical patients subject to considerable excitement, to any activity in the disease, such as quick pulse, high temperature, night fever, and especially a tendency to hœmorrhage, or cases of consumption with bronchial complications, would do well to select Hyères in preference to the ordinary Riviera stations. Innumerable cases might be cited of patients who have come from Nice or Mentone in a state of nervous excitement and wakefulness and who have slept well and soundly at Hyères. Dr Edwin Lee recognizes that the climate of Hyères is more soft, less exciting, and less variable than that of Nice. Dr Clarke in his work on the "Influence of Climate" states that of all the towns of Provence, Hyères offers the most exceptional advantages to persons suffering from chest disease, for it enjoys the mildest climate, and nowhere could patients find a better position. Dr Barth in his report to *les Archives Général deMédicine* considers Nice more cold, damp, and windy, than Hyères. Dr *Opinions of eminent physicians.* de Valcourt points out the injurious effects that result from the immediate neighbourhood of the sea. Dr Fournier considers such towns as Nice dangerous in many cases of phthisis. Dr Darralde, of the Eaux-Bonnes; Dr Carrière, in his work on climate; Dr Foderé, who practiced some time at Nice; Dr Bayle, professor to the Paris Faculty of Medicine; Dr Laure, Dr Sordet, Dr Honoraty, and many other medical men whom it would take too long to enumerate, all concur in recommending Hyères. The celebrated French physicians, Dr. Chomel and Dr. Andrell, the "Princes of Science," as they have been called, sent their patients to Hyères; for undoubtedly the sedative, uniform and healing character of its climate is widely recognized in France. It is, therefore, not too much to say that whereas patients suffering from hœmorrhage find their health often impaired in the excessively dry and exciting places, such as Malaga, Algiers, Nice and most of the Riviera stations, their complaint remains at least in a passive state at Hyères.

Apart from cases of pure phthisis, a winter spent at Hyères will prove of great benefit in bronchitis, bronchial asthma, rheumatism, with bronchial complications, muscular rheumatism, anæmia, chlorosis, functional derangements *The various diseases* and irregularities in women, which are not only so *benefited.* injurious in themselves but often predispose the system to phthisis. Indeed, there are few diseases that will not benefit by the outdoor exercise,the open air which is freely enjoyed precisely during those months, when, in England, it would be necessary to shut the windows, to light fires, and confine the patient in a room that must of necessity become more or less close. For these reasons Hyères may also be recommended in heart disease when there is a great craving for open air, a longing to be out of doors, or at least to throw open the windows. This cannot be done safely in England during the winter, while most of the Riviera stations would be found too exciting for heart disease; but Hyères, it has already been demonstrated, is exempt from this special objection.

Indeed, it will be seen, that there are a number of other diseases, apart from what is vaguely termed consumption, which would be favourably influenced by wintering on this spot; and this fact, though of the greatest importance, has not been sufficiently insisted upon. Most medical men will admit that persons subject to diseases of the kidney are more susceptible to the variations of climate than is the case even with consumptive patients. A few of the more distinguished practitioners in London are now sending their patients to winter in the South when afflicted by this form of disease; but the practice is not yet general. Nevertheless, every one must be aware that the slightest chill affects the kidneys, and the students of medical statistics knows how exceptionally prevalent albuminuria is in England. On the other hand, Dr G. Griffith, after careful and special inquiry, assures me that this illness is unknown among the native population of Hyères. It is impossible to exaggerate the importance of so startling a fact; nor is it surprising, under these circumstances, if, as I have had occasion to witness, the most striking result has been achieved in the treatment of this disease at Hyères. The very special influence of the Hyères climate on bronchial asthma has also been again and recently demonstrated. Last year, two gentlemen who had derived no advantage from a sojourn at Algiers during the greater part of the winter, improved considerably when, in response to the advice of a friend, they came to Hyères, for the remainder of the season.

Not the least of the advantages of this latter town is the presence, not merely of skilled English practitioners, but of a physician (Dr Griffith) who, though an Englishman, has had twenty-one years,' experience of the very peculiar effects of the climate and the special diseases that result therefrom. It must *Local medical experience essential.* be borne in mind that the rules applying to England do not suit a climate such as this. Travellers should be careful not to have prescriptions given them in England made up in the South. What may be taken with impunity at home might be dangerous under these very different climatic influences; precautions that would be absurd in the North are essential here; what we may eat and drink with impunity on the shores of the British Channel would certainly produce severe illness on the coast of the Mediterranean. In medicine, diet, and clothes, special local experience is indispensable not merely to the successful, but, I may even say, and without exaggeration, to the safe treatment of the disease. Stimulants should be taken with the *Diet and clothes.* utmost precaution; the local wines, though cheap, are strong, and the system will only support a very small amount of alcohol in such a climate. In the French cafés, the visi-

, tor will find a number of light beverages that will not compromise his health, such as the fruit syrups, Orgeat or Grenadine, with seltzer water or a *siphon*; a little vermouth with syrup of gum, water, and perhaps a dash of bitters; the Eucalypsinthe of Marseilles make, or in fact any of the lighter drinks that the inhabitants themselves consume. At meals the appetite, far from being indulged, should, on the contrary, be restrained. The dangers of the table d'hôte are manifold; indigestion, sometimes of the worse type, is easily induced, and what may be eaten or drunk with impunity either in Paris or London is likely to cause illness in this semi-tropical climate. Imprudence in this respect has robbed many persons of the good they would otherwise have derived from wintering in the South.

With regard to clothing, special precautions must also be taken. The first essential is to protect the head and the back of the neck thoroughly from the rays of the sun, for sun-stroke even in mid-winter is to be feared. The body also should be protected with woollen cloth suits or flannel under-clothes. It is a great mistake to believe that in a hot climate we can wear thin clothes. The clothes should hang as loosely as possible, but should be thick, so as to ward off the hot rays of the sun, and to enable us to withstand the sudden and great changes of temperature that follows when the sun sets. Also, as the sun is so hot, the shade and interior of the houses are comparatively cold; then the wind is often anything but warm, and hence we are exposed to sudden changes of temperature far greater than anything experienced in England. The difference in England between night and day, between shade and sun—when there is any sun—is only slight, and therefore it is not so necessary to carry wraps and overcoats and other contrivances that are easily taken off and on according to whether we stand in the sun or in the shade, or are exposed to the heat or to the wind. The danger at sunset is especially great. It is much safer to go out at night than to remain out during the period of brusque transition when the sun sinks in the horizon.

All these considerations render local knowledge an essential attribute for a successful practitioner in these Southern resorts, and Dr Griffith has had the longest experience on the Riviera. His partner, Dr Biden, brings to the experience of Dr Griffith *Dr. Griffith* the zeal, the devotion and ardour of youth. In their *& Dr.Biden.* hands, and assisted by the salubrious climate of Hyères, the patient may rest assured that he has obtained the succour of all that nature and art can do for him. Nor will the reader accuse me of unworthy partiality when I add that to the climate of Hyères, and to the untiring attention and skill of our two resident English doctors, is due the preservation from a most dangerous illness of a life that was more dear to me than my own existence. Persons, however, who prefer calling in the assistance of a French doctor, will find a number of skilled practitioners whose addresses are given in the appendix. The reputation of Dr Vidal, for instance, has travelled beyond the confines of Provence, and his cordial, genial manners will help to cheer the sick who resort to his skill.

It should also be noted that Hyères possesses a variety of climates which are most useful in the treatment of disease. There is the climate of Hyères proper, of the town and its immediate surrounding, which has been described at length, and *Variety of* yet it should be noted that the two ends of the town *climates.* differ considerably ; that cases of asthma whether complicated with bronchitis or emphysema generally do better at the West end. It would be well, therefore, before taking rooms or a villa, and definitely settling in any particular quarter to ask the advice of a physician whose local experience is undoubted and of long date. Then we have at Costebelle a different climate altogether. There the balsamic influence of the pine woods, the higher elevation of the ground, and the nearness to the sea are more stimulating and would suit many persons who find Hyères too sedative in its effects. Indeed, patients are sometimes sent from Hyères to Costebelle for a week, as a sort of tonic. Again at the seaside itself, particularly when the works for drying up the marshes near the Plage are completed, an admirable site could be found for the treatment of strumous constitutions. In such cases, the close proximity of the Mediterranean, the excessive saltness of its waters, and the exposure of this position to the strengthening effects of the sea-winds, would be great advantages. Hence at an easy walk from Hyères, we have three very different climates, so that, within the same neighbourhood, diseases fundamentally different in character, and necessary treatment would still derive great benefits from wintering in this favoured spot. Nor need these curative effects be limited to the winter season. At the sea side, in any case, an agreeable summer station might be founded, and the coolness and strengthening character of the sea breezes would afford great relief to those who are accustomed to live inland. At the end of the Plage du Ceinturon, near the Salins des Pesquiers, a spot has been selected for the treatment of strumous disease. It is exposed to every wind, and every wind to reach it must pass over the sea or the salt marshes, with the exception of the North wind, which is the rarest of all winds on this coast. At the same time the site is surrounded *Strumous* by fragrant balsamic pine trees. It has been singled *patients.* out by Dr Vidal as most suited for a hospital where the poor children from the great towns might be sent and might be cured of the strumous taint. As it is, these unfortunate waifs and strays cost the state a large sum, and after all generally die before they are old enough to render any service in exchange for the charity they have received. Here, on the contrary, a radical cure might be effected, thus ensuring a great benefit to humanity and an economy to the public purse. The experiments that have been made in the treatment of this disease on this coast prove that these anticipations are well-founded. Hence we have on this spot firstly a site exposed to every wind, and every wind, with one unimportant exception, bringing with it the saline particles and exciting influence of the Mediterranean sea. Secondly, in the vale of Costebelle, and on the coast towards Carqueyranne, we have another climate warmer by two or three degrees and more bracing than Hyères. Here there is ample shelter from cold winds, but the position is not protected from the exciting influence of the Mediterranean. Thirdly, there is the sedative climate of Hyères itself, already fully described.

With respect to the sanitary condition of Hyères, it would scarcely be fair, now that the town is in a state of transition, to describe the old state of affairs. In the old town, the mortality is undoubtedly very high among the native population, and this is due principally to ignorance and the bad nursing of infants. *Sanitary* *condition.* What is more important to the foreigner and the visitor is the fact that Hyères is free from epidemics. When the cholera raged throughout France it did not come here. Again, after the Franco-German war, in 1871, though a number of soldiers, convalescent from small-pox, were sent to Hyères, this dreaded disease did not take root in the town. This immunity is not the result, it is true, of good sanitation, *Immunity* *from epi-* *demic di-* *sease.* but it exists; and I should be tempted to attribute the fact to the rocky nature of the soil, rendering the filtration of injurious matter difficult, and also to the fact that the dirt is for the most part on the surface; and, however offensive to the senses, is exposed freely to the purifying influence of the sun, the open air and the wind. Further, it must be borne in mind that though nothing can be easier than to criticise the bad sanitation of Hyères, the same objection could with equal justice be raised against any town in the South of France; while in Italy, to judge from all the accounts I have received, the state of affairs is even worse. On the other hand, it should be noted that several proprietors of hotels and villas have displayed considerable ability and energy in seeking to modify these evils. The villa Farnese, not to enter into details, is a perfect ideal of sanitation, and if, even in England, there were many such dwellings, our death-rate would soon be sensibly reduced. At the Hotel de l'Ermitage, the soil is removed every twenty-four hours so that no time is allowed for the process of fermentation to set in. Here, also, the tank for the supply of drinking water is separated from that which supplies the means of flushing the house drains. Again, at the Hotel des Iles d'Or they have adopted the excellent plan of washing all the house and personal linen on the premises, and as all cases of infectious disease would be removed at once to the hospital, there is no danger of the linen becoming impregnated with *Sanitary measures.* fever germs. In summer, also, the carpets are beaten and exposed for a whole day and night to the open air, so that they are cleaned and purified, and the colours revived by the freshening dew. As the climate admits of the windows being opened nearly every day, and for the whole day, this fact alone is a great compensation for a number of sanitary defects. At the same time, it would be well that each visitor should see to the drains of the house he may rent; should make lavish use, on the slightest provocation, of Sporokton, or some other equally powerful combination of disinfecting and deodorizing chemicals, and, above all, lose no opportunity of letting the outer air into his apartments. Finally, I would urge every person who finds any cause of complaint to proceed at once to the Mairie and state his grievance to the Mayor who will be found every morning from ten to eleven o'clock at his office. If more has not been done to improve the sanitation of the town, it is in some measure the consequence of the indolence of visitors who express their dissatisfaction among themselves instead of first complaining to the proper authorities. Nor will any good be achieved by a solitary protest. The complaints must be general and repeated. The authcrities of the town are now becoming alive to the importance of the drainage question, and several leading landowners are agitating actively to obtain great ameliorations.

When sufficient pressure has been thus brought to bear, and energetic action is taken it will be found that Hyères possesses two great and exceptional advantages from a sanitary point of view. First, there is its natural position, the steep inclination of the ground on which it is built, and this will render *Natural hygenic advantages.* the flushing of sewers and the cleaning of streets a very easy matter. Secondly, the town already enjoys an excellent, abundant, and cheap supply of drinking water. * This is derived from an inexhaustible subterranean water bed to the S.E. of the town, and pumped np to an altitude of 301 feet, so that water can be brought even to the villas high up on the side of the hills. This water is consequently drunk at Costebelle as well as in the highest *The water supply.* houses near to Hyères. There is no excuse, therefore, for drinking the more or less contaminated water of the wells which, as usual, are dug dangerously near to the

---

* The following is the official report of the analysis made by the Engineer and Director of the Chimical Laboritory of the Ponts et Chaussées, bearing the date of March 6th, 1876 of the water in queetion.

	Sample A.	Sample B.
Residence of filtration per litre	0,0644	0,0355
Residence of evaporization per litre	0,2718	0,2386

Composition of the Residue obtained by evaporation :—

	Sample A.	Sample B.
Silica	0,0216	0,0198
Sulphuric Acid	0,0371	0,0323
Chlorine	0,0373	0,0202
Alumina and peroxide of iron...	0,0014	0,0018
Lime...	0,0141	0,0108
Magnesia	0,0049	0,0046
Alcali	0,0921	0,0724
Combustible matter	0,0460	0,0300
Carbonic Acid, matter not estimated and lost	0,0166	0,0467
	0,2718	0,2386

cesspool or manure heaps. In the town there are a number of public pumps where the company's pure water can be obtained for nothing and the charge for supplying the interior of the houses is small. Under these circumstances, visitors should enquire, in renting a house, what water is drunk, and give the preference to those places where they will be sure that the supply is pure. Dr Griffith has adopted the excellent plan of forbidding any of his patients to drink any other water than that of the water company. With these simple precautions, the winter may be passed at Hyères without fear, and with much enjoyment. It will be, indeed, difficult to believe that it is the winter, for there are many summers in England when out-door exercise, open windows, and continued fine weather are of rarer occurrence.

THE VEGETATION OF HYÈRES.

CHAPTER III.

Most persons have had to travel hundreds of miles further South in order to experience a transition similar to that which the comparatively short journey to Hyères enables us to enjoy. It is difficult to believe that in France, not more than thirty hours' post from London, while still within the pale of advanced Western civilization, we can live in a semi-tropical climate surrounded by all the marvels of vegetation which are generally associated with distant colonies and semi-barbaric southern countries. There is no better proof of the climatic advantages of Hyères than the vegetation that grows in the open, flowers in the winter, and survives uninjured the coldest months of the year. It is im-

Vegetation a proof of climate advantages. possible to walk a few steps at Hyères without noting the magnificent palm trees, often laden with dates, the yucca, the aloes, the prickly pears, the roses in mid winter, the geraniums, the English summer flowers blooming in the open air during December and January. The fact is, that the border line separating the natural characteristics of one country from those of another region consists, as a rule, of a mountain chain; for it is remarkable how shores that face each other are alike though there may be a broad sea between them. Thus, though the great Atlantic keeps them apart, the shores of Senegambia have often been compared with the land stretching from the Amazon to the Orinoco rivers. In any case, the difference is not so marked as that which can be found at but a small

EUCALYPTUS, VARIETY.

Bud and Blossom.

Garden of Hyères. Published by J. Evans & Company, 11, Bridge St. Westminster, London S.W.

Copyright.

distance inland. The strands of Peru and Chili do not resemble those of Brazil, and it appears as if the same waters, the same marine currents, in shaping distant shores, imparted to them a family likeness. A chain of mountains, on the contrary, constitutes a real barrier, and produces fundamental differences in the climate, vegetation, and, consequently, in the character of the populations. The arid, inaccessible summits of the mountains separate both animal and vegetable life, but the sea, on the contrary, unites more than it divides. It is easier for ships to cross the sea than for caravans or railways to go over mountain passes. Hence it is that the characteristics of France cease when once we reach the mountains that separate the Riviera from the North, and we find on the Southern slopes of this range that the land assumes the aspect of the opposite coast—of Northern Africa. The cork-oak, the umbrella pine, the olive and the palm proclaim on all sides the Eastern or Southern nature of the soil and climate.

Plants, which in the centre of France, in the North, and in England attain but a small size and only flower once in twelve months, become shrubs at Hyères and flower two or three times a year. Other plants, which with us can only be reared in hot houses, grow in the open air throughout the winter, though two degrees of frost would suffice to make the leaves fall and injure the blossom, while the fruit would drop at five degrees, and the plant die if exposed to eight degrees of frost. It is, however, the presence of the semi-tropical vegeta- *Semi tropi-* tion which will immediately and most forcibly *cal vegeta-* impress the visitor; and first among these *tion.* growths, the palm is the most striking to the eye and imagination. In the gardens of private villas, in the main thoroughfare of the town, at the Place des Palmiers, throughout the Avenue des Palmiers, and here and there springing up from field and market garden in the plain of Hyères, the stately, graceful palm lifts its plume-like crest against the blue sky. Nowhere on the French Riviera are the palms so beautiful or so numerous.   Bouche in his "Histoire de Provence" relates with minuteness of detail that on Sunday, the 29th of October, 1564, Henry IV, having slept at the Chateau d' Hyêres the previous evening, proceeded to visit the palm, the orange, and the pepper trees that grew in the neighbourhood.   Probably the Moors, who had already planted their favourite tree throughout Andalusia, also thought to cultivate the palm on the Riviera, and this trace of their occupation survived even in the reign of Henry IV.   At som subsequent date, however, the trees must have been cut down, or have died out, for now the oldest palm at Hyères has not seen more than seventy summers while by far the greater number are not half that age. Nevertheless, the effect already produced is marvellous.

Palm trees.

On all sides there is now a demand for palm trees, and the plant has become an article of commerce as well as one of the most majestic ornaments that can possibly be given to a southern town.   In all the nursery gardens the palm is extensively cultivated, and there are about ten varieties that grow easily at Hyères.   These are generally sold when they have attained the age of four to six years and a height of three to five feet. Their value then varies from four to ten francs.   They can be easily transported and sent any distance by rail.   When the palm grows in size and assumes the proportions of a tree, its value is greatly increased; but even when it is twenty years old it can still be transported.   Twenty such palms were sent from the Jardin Huber to the Paris Exhibition of 1878, and they weighed from 22,000 lbs to 33,000 lbs each, varying in value from £20 to £50 the tree.   It is, however, the risk and cost of removal, rather than the value of the tree, which renders any extensive trade in large palms impracticable.   All the cultivation growing round the large tree has to be destroyed before it can be uprooted.

Trade in palm trees.

A palm tree, worth £120, was sold some years ago to M. Magnier, and removed from Hyères to San Salvador, a few miles distance. This operation cost about £200; for it was necessary to build a special scaffolding to lift the tree, a particular cart had to be constructed to hold it, and fifteen horses were required to drag it along. Further, the gates through which the tree had to pass were destroyed to give room for this monster plant which probably weighed 60,000 lbs! Then four years had to run their course before it could confidently be stated whether the tree would survive this trial. The friends who, on this occasion wagered a dinner as to the success of the transportion had therefore time enough to gain a keen appetite before the verdict was given.

After the palm, the Eucalyptus, or Australian blue gum tree, is a prominent witness to the semi-tropical vegetation of Hyères. These noble and most use- *The Eucalyptus.* ful trees were popularized in this region by M. Ramel, who is now well-known throughout the neighbourhood as the Le Père de l' Eucalyptus. This gentleman had travelled in Australia where he became acquainted with Herr von Müller, the director of the Melbourne botanical garden, and some eighteen years ago brought back to Hyères a large collection of seeds and young plants. Ten years previously, however, M. Dellor, a partner in the firm of Huber and Co., the celebrated horticulturists, had cultivated the Eucalyptus, but it was not then appreciated. The knowledge of its sanitary properties had not been popularized; it was only subsequently discovered that entire villages and districts had been freed from the prevalence of malaria, by the very easy method of planting a number of these trees. It possesses a large quantity of volatile oil, emits a fragrant balsamic odour from stem, leaf, bark, and branch, especially if these are a little bruised. Like the resin of the fir tree this volatile principle is a source of ozone, and many experiments are now made in most of the French hospitals to ascertain its medical qualities. A

pectoral paste for coughs made by distilling freshly picked
leaves of the Eucalyptus is sold at Hyères, and

Its sanitary properties. it is asserted that the mere chewing of a few
leaves will cure a cold in the head almost
instantaneously. Further experiments are required however, to confirm this consoling theory. With respect to
the purification of malarious districts, Dr Arthur Hill Hassall
states that "The Eucalyptus is credited with febrifuge properties; these some would assign to the volatile oil it contains,
and to the action of this as an ozonizer, while others with more
reason attribute its beneficial effects to its drying up, by the
rapidity of its growth and the abundance of its evergreen foliage, the damp, marshy, and even malarious soil in which it is
frequently planted."

All these facts, however, were ignored thirty years ago, and it
was only M. Ramel's more recent attempt to introduce the Eucalyptus tree that proved successful. Now they are planted on the
side of every road, in every garden, and in the course

Its intro- duction. of a few years the result will be magnificent if we
may judge from the comparatively small number
of old trees that exist. The oldest of these trees overshadows
the road to the Jardin d' Acclimatation, and though the seed,
smaller than a pin's head, was planted only twenty three
years ago, the tree has reached an altitude of about fifty
feet, and the stem measures ninety eight inches in circum-
ference. Altogether, there are seventeen varieties of Eucalyptus
cultivated at Hyères, of which the Eucalyptus Globulus is the
most hardy and the most common. Many of the species have
smaller and more delicate leaves, but each possesses the same
peculiar odour.

Mingling with, and growing with equal profusion under the
palms, the Eucalyptus and the Olive trees, the aloes and the cactus
or prickly pears impart a truly Oriental aspect to the scenery. As
in Andalusia, we even meet hedges made of aloes, and the prickly

EUCALYPTUS GLOBULUS.

Leaves and Seed Pods.

Garden of Hyères. Published by J.Evans & Company, 11, Bridge St Westminster, London. S.W

Copyright.

pear ripens in the open air, and can be eaten with pleasure. But they must be handled with care, as the thorns will produce great irritation. They can, however, be safely picked with a piece of paper, laid on a plate and eaten with a knife and fork. The top part, or ring, should be cut off, a longitudinal incision is made through the skin; the pear can then be laid open and the pulpy inside, when scooped out, will be found more refreshing than an orange in hot weather. At Hyères few persons, however, think of eating this very wholesome fruit; though in Andalusia the inhabitants will consume twenty or thirty prickly pears in a day.

The prickly pear, &c.

Orange trees, lemon trees, the false pepper trees, almond trees, all abound, though the cultivation of the former has been abandoned of late. Indeed, nothing pays better than the market garden. Early strawberries, early vegetables, for the Paris and London markets produce the surest and largest incomes; hence even the olive and almond trees are daily cut down to make room for vegetable and strawberry beds. The oranges are still more at a discount, for those which are now so easily imported from Spain are of a much superior quality. All that can be said for the Hyères orange is, that as the visitors can eat it out ripe from the tree, it will be found more refreshing than the oranges that have travelled a considerable distance and ripened in the journey. The fig trees which abound throughout the district produce a far superior fruit, but again the pomegranates cannot be compared with those of Spain. Nevertheless they all testify to the mildness of the climate. This is further demonstrated by the prevalence of evergreens; for these plants, as a rule, possess a thick skin, or cuticle, their moisture cannot therefore evaporate so rapidly, and they are thus able to resist the long droughts and the dryness of the atmosphere. Further, an evergreen does not depend so much on its roots and the surrounding earth for nutriment; but, possessing leaves both summer and winter, is able to nourish itself at all seasons from the atmosphere.

Early fruits and vegetables.

The Cypress tree, the umbrella Pine, and the cork tree are
noble specimens of the evergreens; the former are
The locust tree, &c. planted side by side for the purpose of making high
walls, and so disposed as to shelter the fields
from cold winds. Then we have various species of wild
laurels, with dark green leaves and bunches of blue black
berries. The Carouba or Locust tree (*Ceratonia siliqua*) gives
us not only an abundant evergreen foliage, but a bean-like
pod containing so much sugar and nitrogenous matter that
many persons would find its fruit pleasant food, and argue
that St. John the Baptist might have fared worse when
he lived on locusts and honey in the wilderness. In any
case, the pod is very useful for the rearing of cattle, and has been
exported extensively to England. A good carouba tree is said to
equal an income of sixteen shillings a year, and there is a fine
specimen half way up the hill between the Place de la Rade and
the Chateau d' Hyères. It covers the most barren rocks with rich
foliage, lives almost exclusively by its leaves, for it grows where
there is hardly a speck of soil.

The Lentiscus also with its winter flowers recalls the chief botanical feature of Palestine and Syria, and abounds at
Eastern vegetation. Hyères and its surrounding hills, while lower down
in the plain the golden blossoms of the Acacias
relieve the heavy green of the Oleander. Then there is that
species of Sarsaparilla known as the *Smilax aspera*, that
clambers over trees, clinging like ivy to their boughs, forming a veil, and hiding, notably, the river Gapeau from our
view. Walls of bamboo cane indicate the presence of small water
courses, while the creeping cactus like a huge serpent runs up
walls of cottage or farm. At our feet, in the valley or on the hill-
side, there is an endless variety of wild flowers from
Wild flowers the mauve Anemone to the purple Violet, from the
brown, chocolate coloured, hood shaped Arum, with its
bulbous, nutritious roots to the yellowish green flowers of
the poisonous Euphobia, with its milk-white sap. The Maiden's-

hair fern lines the common ditch wall, the Iris, the Mediterranean heath, the Tulip, the Mignonette, the Hyacinth, a gigantic daisy, the Parma Violet, and innumerable other flowers grow at random on all sides, and the student of botany, the lover of nature, would find here an all-absorbing field for research, where each day's investigation would reveal a new charm, another beautiful or rare plant.

Not only is the country round Hyères exceptionally rich with rare flora, but it would be difficult to find better gardens with choice collections recruited from every part of the world. There are notably the Jardin d' Acclimatation, which is a branch establishment of the celebrated garden in the Bois de Boulogne, at Paris; the Jardin Huber, and the Jardin Denis. All these are open free to the public. The latter *dens.* has been purchased by the Municipality. It is admirably situated behind M. Denis' private house, to the east of the Place de la Rade. This house will probably be pulled down, so that a full view of the garden will be obtained from the square, and it is proposed to build a Casino at the rear. In the meanwhile, the garden is entered by a little door facing the Hotel d' Orient, which cannot be pushed open without shaking the branches of a magnificent fan palm, the Latania borbonica; and close to it we have the *Avocat* tree and a gigantic Japanese medlar. This latter tree, *The Jardin Denis.* bearing a delicious fruit, is to be seen all over Hyères, but they have attained exceptional size in garden. In the same direction a quantity of *Cyperus Papyrus* will be found growing in a little pond. When we remember that it was with this grass the ancient Egyptians made their paper, and that on this *papyrus* we find some of the very earliest records of human civilization extant, it is impossible to look at the plant without feeling some emotion.

In the avenue of Magnolias there is one tree, a Magnolia Gloriosa, the flower of which when opened measured fourteen and a half inches in diameter; but there is nothing more remarkable in

this garden for its wild and truly oriental aspect than the short
avenue of palm trees. These noble trees comp-
Giant Magnolia. letely shade the path. At their roots the smaller
Yucca, the Cycas Revoluta, and other specimens of
tropical vegetation, complete the illusion. Yet these trees,
so Eastern in their aspect, are associated with the history
of Northern France. The third tree to the left, towards
which a huge palm bows in homage, was planted in 1840 by
Lamartine ! The great poet and statesman had brought the date
over from Costebelle to sow it in M. Denis' garden.

Nearer to the house will be found a number of fine Camelias
blooming even in January ; while in an angle between the side of
house and the outer wall, two huge pines intertwine their branches;
the one is the *Pinus Longifolia,* from the Himalaya mountains,
and the other the *Araucaria Cunninghami,* from
Foreign trees. China. The latter has reached an altitude of
about eighty feet ; and by reason of their weird
character, their gigantic size, their truly foreign aspect, these
two trees form one of the most impressive groups of the
garden. Near at hand the *Araucaria Bidwili* from Australia,
is one of the finest specimens on the Riviera, and the *pinus
Canariensis* in front of the house, and a cluster of Madagascar bamboos should be remarked. The gardener, M. Josse, employs these
bamboos for his tools, and so great is their strength that a broom
stick of Madagascar bamboo will support a weight of 308 lbs
without snapping.

The Jardin Huber is larger, laid out with more order, contains
a richer collection of plants, but is not so
The Jardin Huber. picturesque. This garden is better suited for the
study of botany, particularly as the managers have
considerately attached labels to each of the plants. A
beautiful straight avenue faces the main entrance, and our first
step brings us under a green arch formed by the Ephedra creeper
hanging over the Coral tree and hiding its branches. This long
hairy growth has often been called Aaron's beard, a simile which

TROPICAL PLANTS IN THE JARDIN HUBER

Dracaena Indivisa.   *Yucca Filifera in Full Bloom.*
            Aloe in Flower.
            Cycas revoluta.

Garden of Hyères. Published by J. Evans & Company, 11, Bridge S.t Westminster, London. S.W is readily appreciated. A few lovely flower trees, the scarlet *Salvia Cardinalis*, the golden Acacias, of which there are eighty or ninety varieties, line the road on either side till we reach the remarkable group of semi-tropical plants that forms the subject of our illustration. The tall pole of an aloe in full blossom is the centre piece. Indeed, throughout the whole district, aloes in full bloom will be found in abundance. The gigantic *Yucca filifera* which recently blossomed and gave good seed, is far more remarkable ; and *Dracœna indivisa* and the many bladed *Cycas revoluta* help to complete one of the most striking groups of exotic vegetation that can be seen anywhere. It is a powerful illustration of the climate of Hyères, and when we contemplate the surrounding plants, the sun-lit, brilliant, olive clad hill in the back ground, it is almost impossible to believe that we are still in the West of Europe. Have we not close at hand, two gigantic Banana trees, near to the thorny, leafless, dark green orange *Trees from all parts.* tree of Japan with its snow white blossoms, the Cocoa fruit tree of the Brazils with its fruit ripening under its curved and graceful branches. A magnificent pine from the Canary islands shelters the Japanese Aralia, a green plant which, by reason of the odd shape of its leaves reminds us forcibly of Japanese designs and tea trays ; a huge tree from Nepaul intertwines its branches with another giant from California ; the Kennedya creeper covers the garden wall with its delicate lilac spray ; a Cypress from a Chinese cemetery nods a fraternal salutation to the Cypress of the Western climes ; and, at a lower level, the *Hibuscus Mutabilis* puts forth its white flower that blushes pink on the second day of its existence and becomes a bold red on the third day. The Bottle tree with its bright green stem, and the South American tree that provides the wood for the manufacture of guitars are also close at hand ; and, as a startling exception to the general character of the growths in this garden, we find a pine from the Sierra Nevada of Spain (the *Absis Pinsapo*), a tree accustomed to the snow of those cold altitudes.

Following the wall to the right of the principal entrance, what
is perhaps the most curious tree of the garden will be found. It
has a thick triangular leaf with a thorn at the apex of each angle.
The branches and leaves are all stiff and cannot bend to the wind.
The colour, the firmness, the rigidity of the tree would make many

Rare plants

persons question if it be not some grotesque,
metallic imitatation. It is a real tree, nevertheless,
and grows in Chili, where, in consequence of its thorny
disposition, the discoverer named it after M. Collet, one of
his very excellent but very bad tempered friends ; hence it is
now known as the Colletia du Chili, and the visitor should
beware not to stumble against this very formidable agglomeration
of pricks. Looking also somewhat formidable, we meet in
different parts of the garden a circular plant that throws
out direct from the ground about three hundred long leaves like
rapier blades with spiked edges. This is the *Dasylirion Longi-
folium*, and each plant is worth about £2. But we have here
also another species in which the blades, about two inches broad
and a yard and a half long, are quite smooth, like a luxuriant
silky, gigantic grass, and these are worth £20 to £25 each—a
rare plant therefore.

From the Jardin Huber seeds and plants are exported to all
parts of the world; as also from the establishment of Monsieur
Nardy. The garden of the latter gentleman is more like a nursery,
where excellent plants are reared, but it is not laid out for visitors
to inspect. The same may be said of the Jardin Beauregard,
which stretches out into the plain from the foot

*Cut flowers
for England*

of the Place des Palmiers. All flowers used for
ornamentation, bouquets, &c., are extensively cultivated in these gardens ; and for a franc and upwards boxes
containing 250 grammes of choice flowers are sold to visitors
who desire to send them by post to friends abroad. Larger
quantities for Paris and for Covent Garden are dispatched
every day by express, together with innumerable trees packed in a
wonderful manner, and that travel safely thousands of miles. Thus

it is not without reason that we speak in preference of the garden of Hyères rather than of the town of Hyères, for it is as a garden more than in any other respect that this favoured spot has acquired its renown and won the affection of its residents and visitors.

———

THE NATURAL SCIENCES AT HYÈRES.

CHAPTER IV.

Of all the visitors to Hyères none are so content as those who
have the good fortune to love one or more of the natural
sciences which can be studied with so much advantage in this
neighbourhood. They supply a motive for numerous excursions
over the most entrancing country, and increase the attraction of
every walk so that it is impossible to tire of a combination of
magnificent scenery with the absorbing interest of scientific
research. There are at Hyères many persons who as botanists,
as students of Entomology find their life one long, glad song, their
character is gradually softened by the sublime contemplation of
nature's harmonies, the grandeur of nature's scheme enables than

*Independ-
ent happi-
ness.* to look down from a lofty height on the petty
squabbles of humanity, and, as their enjoyment does
not depend on fortune or on the world's approba

tion they lead a life of independent happiness, which is rendered all the more intense by the good health they derive
from their constant out-door exercise. Indeed I would earn-
estly advise anyone who is condemned by circumstances or
by his doctor to spend a winter or several winters at Hyères, to
select a science and devote himself to its study. In the chapter on
vegetation enough, perhaps, has been said to indicate how broad
is that field of observation and how great and exceptional are the
climatic advantages in this respect. But if geology, zoology or
entomology are preferred, Hyères also offers special attractions.
Even with respect to mineralogy there are here some points of
interest though no mines are now worked.

Excursionists to Carqueyranne are often recommended to visit the copper deposits, to the extreme west of the Commune of Hyères. There is another similar deposit on the road from Saint Martin and la Maunière ; but there is not a very large accumulation of this metal. There is also much iron near Pomponiana, and many curious crystalizations of oxidated iron. The sulphuretted antimony which can be found in the Maures *Mineralogy.* mountains is, however, of greater importance; especially at the Bastide du Charbonnier, near Notre Dames des Maures where it is mixed with a little zinc and sulphate of lead. Some fine aluminous silicates combined with a small quantity of bioxide of iron are to be picked up in the islands. The asbestos, the quartz and feldspar, actinolites, and a number of other interesting formations may be unearthed in the mountains, and more especially in the Iles d'Or.

To the geologist these islands will be the first object of enquiry. Then he will wish to visit Six-Fours and Toulon, to trace the ancient bed of the Gapeau and compare it with its modern course. There are three distinct formations. The calcareous mountains, notably the Faron and the Coudon that protect Toulon, then the granatic Maures mountains, with their magnificent vegetation of umbrella pines and the cork oak, and finally the eruptive rocks of the Esterel chain. These three geological groups *Geology.* are thoroughly distinct one from another. They not only differ in age but in general outline, in their vegetation and in their colour. The grey tints of the Faron, present a forcible contrast to the sombre green of the eternal forests that clothe the Maures mountains, and flaming red porphyry of the Esterel chain ; but each colour only adds new grandeur to the brilliant blue of the Mediterranean and the dazzling white of its foam. The islands, it will be seen at once, are but a detachment of the Maures chain. The presque'ile de Gien, of course, has only been recently joined to the main land, and when in 1811, inundations afflicted the country, the new link was carried away, and has since been rebuilt artificially and at great cost.

De Saussure describes how he sailed round these islands in a little boat, examining the nature of each rock and tracing its history back through hundreds of centuries. It would take too much space to give even a summary of such researches, but the mere fact that De Saussure lingered here for so long will perhaps suffice to convince the geologist that he will find near Hyères ample material with which to occupy his powers of research. M. Pareto's works should also be procured, for he was commissioned to study the geology of these coasts; while M. Lentheric gives us a most powerful summary of the general aspect and history of the country. The chain of the Maures mountains which shelter Hyères corresponds with the mountains to the south-east of France, its vegetation recalls the splendid forests of the Vosges and the Ardennes, while its rocks remind us of the granitic up-heavings that constitute the island of Corsica. It was these hills that formed the barrier to the ancient sea that rolled over the now fertile plains of France. They existed before Europe came into being, and their history is therefore of the most ancient.

The Maures and the Esterel formed islands or series of islands during the many centuries which preceded the stratified formation of the present crust of the earth. M. Lentheric argues that when the earth had cooled a little it received deluges of rain, due to the condensation of the thick vapours that enveloped it with humid atmosphere. The *Geological history.* primitive sea occupied the greater part of the spot now known as Europe. All the space stretching between Spain and the Aural mountains was below water. What ultimately became Gaul was then but a sea with two bare, uncultivated, and absolutely desert islands. The one consisted of the granite rocks of Brittany and the Vendée; the other was the central table-land of Auvergne. More to the south there were two islands lost in the seas; the one the Maures, the other the Esterel. Vegetable and animal life did not yet exist, and the first organisms were only able to develop themselves at a much later period, and leave their fragments on the lands slowly formed by the deposits of the great Silurian sea. With the exception of some slight modifications, the outline of this primitive sea, which has varied so greatly in other parts of our territory has remained almost the same on the southern slope of the Maures range ; and the rocky coast stretching from Hyères to Fréjus presents the same design, the same cuttings, as during that most 'ancient period which geologists call the "period of transition," and which we may without hesitation consider many thousands of centuries old. This period was the immediate precursor of the immense calcareous formations out of which the greater part of our land is formed. Thus for an incalculable length of time the sea has beaten up against this wall of granite, has gnawed at these precipitous cliffs, and with difficulty rounded off some of the points, and thus very slowly formed those soft beaches of Cavalaire Bormes, Saint Tropez, etc. When therefore, following the northern shores of the Mediterranean we contemplate the verdant slopes of the Montagnes Maures, or the ardent red of the rocky Esterel, we may reflect with feelings of awe that these hills existed before animal life came into being !—while the land of France had not yet been formed, while the silent waters reigned supreme over what is now the bed of human civilzation !

The Mediterranean will irresistably attract the lover of nature. The special character of its waters, its vegetable and animal life differing so greatly from those of the Atlantic, cannot fail to interest. The invalid will probably experience a sense of disappointment when he misses the fresh stimulating scent so remarkable on the shores of the Atlantic. This feature is due first to the absence of trade winds, but more especially to the fact that the Mediterranean water only contains 5 per cent of suspended oxygen, while the proportion in the water of the Atlantic is as much as 20 per cent. The result is that not only does this water fail to impart a special fragrance to the air, but it cannot nourish many fish. The exceptional warmth of the water is also an *The Mediterranean.* obstacle to the development of fish. Our most prolific

tribes, the cod, sole, mackerel, herring all come from northern lati-
tudes, they follow the colder sea currents, and are not to
be found in the warm Mediterranean. If, however, the fish
are rare they are perhaps all the more curious, and on one
occasion two devil fish were caught off Nice. These anti-
deluvian monsters weighed respectively 1328 and 885 pounds !
Coral and spunge line the deep, and are still sought by
the Genoese fishermen. Tunny fish, *thynnus*, are often
caught weighing 400 lbs. A species of the beautiful tropical
Bonito, the *Pelamys Sarda*, twenty to thirty inches in length,
and other similar species may be caught ; while, of course, the
Bouillabaise and sardines fish are daily consumed. Indeed, the
epicure as well as the naturalist will find much to interest him in
the very peculiar character of the Mediterranean fisheries.

The ornithologist will also meet rare subjects near the coast ;
and notably the Golden Oriole, the Huppoo, some handsome Wood-
Ornithology peckers and the Bee-eater. Then there are innumerable migratory tribes that come from the north to
winter on the Riviera ; the redbreast, the wren, the wagtail
thrushes, blackbirds, larks, gold finches, linnets, and other familiar
friends all flock down from our own latitude to enjoy the milder
winter on the Mediterranean.

Reptiles on their side do not fail to benefit by the climate.
Lizards run about freely in the winter. There is one huge,
Lizard, the Jeco, some ten inches in length, grey in colour with
white stars, which, together with the Oselata, is special to the
South. The latter is of a dark green with white and blue pearl
like marks that are greatly admired. These graceful and
beautiful animals are quite inoffensive. They live on insects, and
the most harm they can do is to weaken the strength of the walls in
which they pierce their dwelling holes. If in self-defence they bite
the persons who capture them the bite is but a nip and altogether
Reptiles free from poison. It is from April to October that these
two remarkable lizards may be seen. The inhabitants

of Hyères are acquainted with twelve different sorts of snakes; but these also, I am assured, are quite free from venom, and need not inspire any fear. Indeed the country round Hyères is even safer than England, for our own poisonous adder is unknown in this dry district. There are, it is true, some scorpions, but their bites only produce slight inflammation, and none of the serious consequences familiar to travellers in the tropics. The Couleuvre Collier, is a specialty of Hyères, and is so named after the dirty whitish yellow collar which encircles the neck of this snake. Nor should . I omit to mention the green tree frog, that makes its presence known in early spring by its lusty croaking. The French visitors often capture this inert animal, and utilise its instinct as a reliable and cheap substitute for a barometer. The frog is put in a glass jar and when the condition of the atmosphere indicates fine weather this sensitive animal finds enough energy to clamber up the leaves sticks or little ladder placed within his prison house. If on the contrary rain is expected he will at once subside to the bottom of his cell.

Entomologists also, even in the keenest winter months will find much to occupy their time. The severest winters have not prevented a number of butterflies from hovering over the flowers that still bloom in spite of the season. During December and January, the Painted Lady (Pyrameis Cardui); the Red-Admiral (Pyrameis Atalanta); and the humming bird, hawk moth are to be seen. Towards the end of February the new year *Entomology* butterflies begin to appear, notably the large and small garden white, the *Rhamni* or brimstone; while in the beginning of April the swallow tail, and a number of other beautiful insects, people the woods and fields. Yet in England, at this season, there is scarcely a single butterfly to be seen. Unfortunately the mildness of the climate encourages not only the existence of the ornamental butterfly, but also of the vexatious mosquito. These abound from May to October or November, being more troublesome in the latter than in the former month, and are serious impediments to true enjoyment of climate and scenery. Nor has any

very satisfactory treatment been prescribed to cure the effect of
the bites. The local common soap, the Marseilles soap, made with
olive oil is considered very efficacious by some persons ; ammonia,
Mosquitoes soda, vinegar, chloroform, oil of cinnamon, or of cloves
are recommended by others. It seems certain that the
result varies according to the constitution of those who use them;
and I should advise giving each a fair trial, while seeking above all
things to avoid the bite itself, on the principle that prevention is
better than cure. For this purpose wire gauze windows, mosquito
curtains, and crushed eucalyptus leaves are most efficacious.
Pastilles of nitrate of potash, burnt at night, have also been found
a good means of driving the troublesome insects away. At Hyères
the inhabitants light huge bon fires in the streets during the summer to burn the mosquitoes and prevent their approaching the
house windows.

The praying mantis, the trap-door spider, the processional
caterpillar, the huge flying grasshopper and the fire fly are all
to be found at Hyères ; the latter may be seen lighting up the
olive groves with bright sparks during the quiet evenings.

The naturalist who is specially interested in doubled winged
insects, whose horny upper wings serve as a rudder to steer with
while the light under wings are used to propel their somewhat
heavy bodies through the air,—the coleopterist, in a word, will find
incomparable advantages at Hyères. There are four distinct fields
of research. The sandy beach, the marsh lands, the mountain side,
Coleoptology and the fruitful highly cultivated plain. Over and above
all this, there is the dark Grotte des Fées where a blind
insect, the anophtalma raymondi, a small species of the carabus tribe,
lives and lives here alone, for the same insect cannot be found in any
other part of the world. On the sands, after sunset, during
March and April, the entomologist will enjoy the rare fortune of
capturing the callienemis latreillei and the saprimus tridens. On
these shores he will find many insects which were originally
natives of China as also the Phytosus Balticus that somehow has
been imported from the north-western shores of Russia ! To the

connoisseur, the marshes are equally interesting, and it suffices to mention that there are many fine Carabus Clathratus, and the Vagans, etc. On the hill sides various Agapanthia, Blabinotus and notably the Foudrasi are to be found. In the cultivated plains the Thelephores, the Elater, the Apionide, and a number of Antichus ; while at St. Mandrier there is a handsome variety of the Julodis Onopordi which has never been seen elsewhere out of Algeria. Apart, also, from the local species, all the insects of the northern and central counties of France can be found in the neighbourhood, and the country has therefore attracted a great number of naturalists who have made rich collections in an incredibly short space of time. In this, however, many persons are indebted to the very able and courteous assistance rendered to them by Captain de Fargues, an indefatigable and enthusiastic coleopterist. For many years this gentleman has carefully noted date and place where he has made any valuable capture or discovery, and is willing, from pure love of his science, to place the fruit of these researches at the disposal of any visitor, telling him day by day exactly where and how he may find rare specimens.

Such, in a few words, are some of the inducements which Hyères offers to the scientific student of nature. Volumes might be written on this subject, and in so brief a chapter it is impossible to do more than touch in a very imperfect manner on some of the leading phases of this vast question; but perhaps sufficient has been said to give a faint indication of the glorious vista opening out to the fortunate persons possessing at least some slight knowledge and the power of appreciating the endless glories of nature's handiwork.

———

THE HISTORY OF HYÈRES.

CHAPTER V.

The past history of Hyères is at once vague and uninteresting. When we consider the number of centuries over which this history ranges, that there are traces of habitation more than three thousand years old, the record of incidents of interest or importance is limited. Implements typical of the age of stone and of bronze have been found throughout the whole neighbourhood,

Archæology and many of these are remarkably fine specimens. The fragments of Celtic pottery and brickwork are numerous, while the ground is absolutely littered with Roman pottery, medals, and even statuary and objects of art. Many of these have been collected by the Duc de Luynes, by M. Parent, and other archæologists ; and some fine specimens, especially of the age of stone and of bronze, may be seen in ¡Dr Griffith's consulting room.

The advent on the coasts of Provence of the Phœnicians, Greeks, and Romans brought about a great confusion in the customs of the inhabitants, and blended the superstitions of the North with those of the South. Still, it is easy to recognise a universal worship of Hercules, who was not only the god of force, but whether looked upon as the Egyptian Baal, the Phœnician Milkarth, or the Thor whom our own forefathers adored, Hercules was also the travelling and conquering god, the founder of towns, the divinity who extended the bounds of the earth. The stone axe placed under the head, in the tomb of the Gaul is the emblem of the Druidic

Ancient Superstition. faith which has not yet entirely died out. It is to be found in tombs dating from the period when bronze and iron weapons were used, and this shows that the stone axe was a talisman, and not an every day implement. It recalled the ancient divinity armed with a stone axe before the use of metal was discovered, and who protected the dead from evil spirits. Nor must it be thought that the variety of religions which have reigned over this land have entirely obliterated the far more ancient beliefs of the Celts. Even in this, the nineteenth century, when a peasant finds one of these stone axes, he will lift it reverently from the ground and hold it to the head of his sick sheep. He is, doubtless, sublimely ignorant as to the tenets of the Druidical faith, but has, nevertheless, unconsciously retained a vague belief in the power of the god Thor to protect his sheep.

History gives no precise or reliable facts as to the foundation of the actual town of Hyères. Probably when Pomponiana was flourishing in all its glory, the Romans built a number of villas at the foot of the hill that shelters Hyères. The quadrangular shape of the towers that still remain on this hill, the thickness of the walls, the manner of fixing the stones in the groin, the "fish" or "herring-bone" style of masonry, bear the peculiar stamp of the fifth century; but there is no written document to prove the existence of any such fortress before the tenth century.

It had then, however, already acquired the reputation *Earliest Records.* of an important stronghold, and belonged to the Comtes de Fos. For several generations this family seem to have governed Hyères, but their rights were ultimately disputed by Charles d'Anjou, the brother of Saint Louis, when he became Comte de Provence. A siege ensued, the house of Fos fought with heroism, and finally a compromise was effected in 1257. The castle and town were surrendered up to the Comtes de Provence, and a sum of money and other lands given to the Comtes de Fos in exchange. Two centuries later, Hyères, together with the rest of Provence, was united to the crown of France.

In the meanwhile Hyères, in common with the whole of the Riviera, had suffered greatly from the inroads of the Moors with out deriving its full share of benefits from these highly civilized invaders. It is generally believed that, not to mention smaller expeditions, the Moors made five great invasions North of the Pyrenees, and in 725 had not only conquered all the Southern towns, but took Autun and trampled over the entire region from the Garonne to the Alps. Their successes, however, carried them

The Moors too far. Weakened by the extent of their domains, Charles Martel and the Franks were, in 732, able to gain their celebrated victory at Poictiers, which ended in the Saracens being entirely driven out of France in 759. Long after this date, however, the coasts of Provence were exposed to their attacks. This insecurity was so great that Charlemagne himself had to undertake a campaign along the Riviera; but his victories were only a temporary advantage. In 846, the Moors again returned and ravaged the entire district, from Genoa to Marseilles. Masters of the sea and of the islands off the coasts, they intercepted all the communications between France and Italy.

M. Lentheric relates that one of their captains, wrecked at St. Tropez, found refuge in the neighbouring mountains, and was so impressed with their strategical importance that he called them "Les Maures." The Moors did not fail to take the hint, and at once occupied these heights, built castles on the summits, and were well protected by the valley of the Argens, the Aille and the Gapeau. This country was soon called the *Pays des Maures*, and the chain of mountains familiar to all travellers along the Mediterranean coast thus derived its present name. The principal stronghold was at *la Garde-Freinet*, where the Moorish remains still

The Mountains of the Moors. exist. But on every hill the Moors established a fort, called in Provencal *fraxinets*, and kept up communications with each other by smoke signals during the day and fires at night. The Moors then began to govern the country in earnest, they received tribute from the native population, and administered justice and settled all disputes. Doubtless they would soon have converted Provence into a second Andalusia. They might have transformed and regenerated by agriculture and irrigation the plain of Arles as they had done the plains of Valencia and Grenada; and certainly they did attempt to work some copper and lead mines in the Alpes Maritimes. Their hold on Provence was, however, too precarious, and they were so often engaged in fighting that they had no time to develope the arts of peace.

The Moors were finally overthrown in 972, when Saint Marjeul, Abbot of Cluny, and Guillaume I, Count of Provence, undertook a crusade against them. Their head quarters, the Grand Fraxinet, was then destroyed; and all their subsequent descents on these coasts partook rather the character of piratical inroads, and can scarcely be qualified as invasions. Nevertheless, the Moors, though conquered, were not exterminated. Those who had married and settled down on the Riviera, were *Expulsion of the Moors* maintained in a state of servitude; and in a will dated as recently as 1250, there is a stipulation that the "Saracens, both men and women, of Villeneuve," should be sold; thus showing that up to this date they formed a distinct section of the population. In fact, the lineal descendants of the Moors are still to be seen in Provence, especially in the valleys of the Maure and Esterel mountains. The angular features, the black eyes, the receding forehead, the crisp hair, even after a lapse of eight centuries, proclaim that the Moorish blood has not yet died out among the inhabitants of Provence.

The presence of the Moors on the Riviera generally, and at Hyères in particular, is a fact which will interest all lovers of the philosophy of history; for, as M. Lentheric observes, we must never forget that it was they who first established a continual exchange of ideas and products between all sorts of different races, who had been more separated by ignorance than by seas and continents. Whatever their motives, the incontestable result of their audacious enterprises was the dis. *Civilising Influence.* closure of horizons to the semi-barbarous peoples of the West, which had previously been concealed from their view, and the opening out of roads that were almost unknown.

The field of history was enlarged by the Moors, and the development of the intellectual life of humanity was the direct consequence of this fusion between Young Europe and the Old East.

These considerations did not, however, prevent the inhabitants of Hyères giving good welcome to St. Louis when he returned from his crusade against the Saracens in Palestine. According to Joinville's Memoirs, the king arrived " in the fort of Hyères and before the castle ; "—a statement which is often quoted to prove that the sea then covered the plain of Hyères. His fleet had taken two months to perform a journey which is now accomplished in less than five days, and arrived at last on the coasts of France in a somewhat dismal condition. The Comte de Fos, who was still in possession of the castle, hoisted the banner of France on the dungeon tower, and in response to this sign of welcome the king landed. The people of Hyères seemed sensible of the honour thus conferred upon them. The clergy in their richest robes, and the whole population came on the beach to meet the saintly king.

St. Louis lands at Hyères. They offered him a place under the dais, but, with characteristic modesty, the king refused to step under the shelter provided for the Host, protesting that such honours in this world could only be addressed to the Almighty. The king then proceeded at once to the the church of the Cordeliers and partook of the Holy Communion. In this ancient building, which is now called the church of St. Louis, a picture of the landing of the king may be seen. When at the castle, Saint Louis sent for a celebrated Cordelier preacher, who, after telling the king some hard truths, refused to join his court, as such surroundings were not fitted to a servant of God. In all these circumstances Saint Louis displayed much real piety, and the Comte de Fos unmeasured hospitality. The king, however, had to hasten to Aix, and from thence to Paris.

After this and for centuries, nothing of importance occurred at Hyères. There were, of course, a number of disputes, and, as usual, many were based on religion and superstition. In 1435,

two unfortunate witches were burnt on the Place
Massillon. They were accused of muttering strange *Witchcroft*
words when they opened a purse, and having thus caused a
married couple to quarrel. Absurd as this may seem, the two
women were burnt alive with the high sanction of the clergy,
who surrounded the stake and chanted hymns. The purse was
also found, and religiously consigned to the flames.

While the Christians were thus disgracing the "religion of
humanity," the Mahommedans had again resumed their depreda-
tions ; and, from 1408 to 1505, constantly attacked the coasts.
So great was the damage they accomplished that the Knights of
St. John had determined to occupy the isle of Porquerolles, the
better to resist the attacks of the Infidels. Charles Quint fearing,
however, that this would give too much influence to the rival
kingdom of France, gave over the island of Malta to this order.
But the Saracens were not to be intimidated by *The Moors*
either the Knights of St. John, Charles Quint, or *Return.*
François I., for, in 1530, they actually landed at Toulon, and
were so far supposed to have destroyed the population that,
when the Christians retook the town, some of the inhabitants
of Hyères were sent to Toulon to repopulate its deserted
streets. A few years later saw the fleet of Charles Quint
anchoring in front of Hyères, and then, subsequently,
François I., finding he had need of all his troops, with-
drew his garrison from the island of Porquerolles, converted it into
a Marquisate, and gave the owner the right of asylum, which was
extended even to criminals ; a circumstance that did not fail to
retard the development of civilization on these coasts. It was
not till the reign of Louis XIV, that the bands of thieves who
naturally collected here were attacked and abolished.

Hyères was now destined to be involved in the wars of religion,
which for so long disturbed the whole of France. In 1564, the
King of Navarre, who subsequently became Henry IV of France,
visited Hyères, and many anecdotes are related concerning the
orange trees planted on his road, the fountains of orange flower water

that distributed fragrant perfume on his passage, of the magnificent palm trees and the carouba and pepper trees which the future king so much admired. Indeed, the vegetation so impressed the queen mother, Catherine de Medicis, that she decided to establish at Hyères a garden for her son Charles ; but the subsequent massacre of St. Bartholomew prevented the execution of this plan. So large were the orange trees that it is related Charles IX, and his brother, the king of Navarre, attempted in vain to embrace the trunk of one of these noble plants, which bore at the time about 14,000 oranges. *" Caroli Regis amplexu glorior "* was engraved on this trunk in commemoration of the event.

Henry IV.

Instead, however, of profiting by the advantages which nature has never ceased to bestow on this favoured district, the inhabitants were first decimated by the plague, and then by civil war. The Baron de Menouillon, who held the Castle of Hyères, was devoted to the cause of the Duke of Savoy. Thereupon the castle was besieged. The town was in favour of Henry IV ; the castle held out for the league, but the fighting was of a mild description. The castle was able to bombard the town, while the town could starve the castle, so that both parties, though maintaining a hostile attitude, nevertheless effected a tacit compromise. Yet, when after a considerable lapse of time, the besiegers were informed, by treachery, that the governor of the castle dined in a particular room, they could not resist the temptation of sending a cannon ball through the window to disturb him at his meal, and this so infuriated the commander that he discharged the whole of his artillery against the town. The fight was evidently beginning in earnest, and this suggested, according to the customs of the times, the propriety of negociating. An envoy was dispatched to the castle, his speech was so eloquent that many officers began to relent, and a capitulation was signed.

The Town against the the Castle.

A few years later M. de Signans was appointed commander of the citadel, but he proved to be unfaithful to the cause of Henry IV ; and, probably by accident, his own father, M. de Grésil, received orders to besiege the fort. This intimate relationship between the rival commanders did not in any way mitigate the horrors of the war. The father was perhaps pleased with this opportunity of once more gaining *Father against Son.* ascendancy over his son; and in any case, both resolved to show that no family consideration would check them in the execution of what they conceived to be their public duties. An attempt to surprise the castle at night signally failed. The drama was not to end here. A flag of truce was hoisted, and M. de Grésil entered the citadel to negociate terms of peace ; but, respecting neither the grey hairs of the old veteran soldier nor the sanctity of a truce, the gates were closed upon him, and M. de Signans constituted himself his own father's jailer ! This and other atrocities caused such a feeling of repulsion among the inhabitants of the town that they became more and more devoted to Henry IV, and more violently opposed to the governor of the castle. At last, in 1596, M. de Fanges, in obedience to the Duc de Guise, whom Henry IV. had appointed governor of Provence, came to besiege the fortress. On this occasion the struggle was most severe, and it was prolonged with varied fortunes for five months, when, happily, the conclusion of a general peace put an end to the contest. The town had been nearly destroyed by the artillery of the castle ; on all sides nothing could be seen but signs of ruin and death ; and yet, when the garrison of the fort marched out in front of the king's troops, they still shouted *Vivo la masso, muort eys bigarrats.* Perhaps it was the fear that this fanaticism would lead to further disturbance which *Destruction of the Castle.* suggested the destruction of all the fortresses where the League had resisted the king. In all cases, the castle of Hyères, partially destroyed after its last siege, was finally levelled to the ground in 1620 ; and with this ends the history of Hyères as an important fortress taking its part in the political events of the day. Cardinal Richelieu had some idea of resuscitating the place from a military point of view, and it was actually visited by Louis XIV., but the plan fell through. The inhabitants also distinguished themselves in resisting an unjust salt tax in 1664 ; and the neighbourhood once more became the scene of contests during the war between Prince Eugène and the King of France.

During the memorable siege of Toulon, in 1707, conducted by the combined Dutch and English fleets, the Duke of Savoy and Prince Eugène, Hyères was used as a hospital for the wounded and the sick ; and it is said they were well treated even when the invading army was compelled to retreat and leave them at the mercy of the inhabitants. After this nothing very special can be said as to the town of Hyères. Its history was merged with that of Toulon during the events of the revolution, and it would take too much space to describe the attitude it assumed with respect to the various factions which were founded during the great revolutionary period, and which still divide the state.

Siege of Toulon.

CASTLE AND CITY WALLS.

Copyright

THE OLD TOWN AND ITS CASTLE.

CHAPTER VI.

All the hotels of Hyères, the English quarter, the villas, the boarding houses, all that is fashionable and commodious is situated outside the old city walls. The historic town, with its archæological associations, its picturesque steep winding streets, its insalubrious odours, its sheltered nooks, its magnificent perspective, is unfrequented by the ordinary visitor, is inhabited but by the humbler classes of the native population, and by the smaller tradesmen, who cater to their wants. This is the more unfortunate as the old town of Hyères really occupies the most sheltered and favoured site of the neighbourhood ; while, on the other hand, the newly created English quarter is more exposed to the mistral than any other part of the town. At the same time, it must be borne in mind that the mistral is a purifying wind, it com- *The Old Town.* pels the invalid to stop in doors, but it oxydises the germs of fever, and reduces the danger of epidemic disease. In the old town, on the contrary, the death rate is high, bad drainage and dirty streets contributing to render the habitations unwholesome. These considerations will not, however, prevent those who take an intelligent interest in the travels they are able to enjoy, from visiting this part of Hyères. Unfortunately the experience will only inspire feelings of regret, for on all sides there are traces of the handsome town that once stood on this spot, and which have been destroyed by the spirit of ignorant Vandalism.

The growth of Hyères can still be easily shown. At the foot
of the ancient castle there was, in the time of Charles of Anjou,
a small town well protected by ramparts that can still be easily
traced. The second and more modern line of ramparts came
down as far as the present main street or Route Nationale, commencing at the place des Palmiers, and extending to the place de
la Rade. Following this course, we will find the porte de
Fenouillet almost intact, but with a big three storied white com-
The Old Gates. monplace house built on the top of it. This speaks well
for the strength of the gate, but scarcely as well for the
architect who thus desecrated an historical monument. The next gate
was the Porte Portalet, the place where it stood still bears the name,
it faces the road to the station while at its back runs the rue
Portalet, which is the chief street for shops in the old town, and
leads directly to the market place, the Hotel de Ville and the
Commissariat of Police. Immediately after the place Portalet we
have the Maison Couture, a modern building with three balconies
standing by one of the ancient square towers. These balconies are
entirely covered with the glycine creeper, which in March conceals
the house under a cascade of magnificent lilac flowers. This lasts
for about three weeks, and is one of the sights of Hyères. At the
place de la Rade we come to the south-east extremity of the old
town, and here, at the corner, remains the ancient gate leading to
the salt marshes, and called the Porte des Salins, which has also
been built over with houses ; but it nevertheless retains much of
its picturesque aspect. The Place de la Rade is the general meet-
ing place of the town. Here are held the fairs; here, on Sundays
and holidays, people congregate and gossip. Close at hand, in the
Place de Strasbourg there is the game of ball, the theatre, and a
dancing establishment at the Café de Paris, while in the Place de
la République the Church of St. Louis is the most frequented
of the town. These three squares all open one into the other, on
all sides there are cafés and buvettes, where tradesmen, artisans
and peasants congregate. In the afternoon, on feasts days and
Sundays, the peasant girls and garden women, when once they

PORTE DU FENOUILLET.

Copyright.

ANCIENT PORTE DES SALINS.

The Garden of Hyères. Published by J. Evans & Company, 11, Bridge St. Westminster. S.W.

have completed their devotions at the neighbouring church, proceed to the dancing room in the place de Stras- *Sunday* bourg, where a band strikes up, and the innocent *Dancing.* fun of a vigorous dance is organised. The gaiety, the sobriety, the good behaviour, the industrial classes display on the occasion of these Sunday afternoon dances, cannot fail to impress the Englishman, accustomed to the rough horse-play and drunkenness he would witness in England if assisting at a similar gathering. The clergy, of course, encourage this innocent amusement, and the proximity of the church with the dancing establishment is of mutual advantage. This close combination of duty and pleasure increases the number of the congregation; while, on the other hand, there is no prospect of the dancing degenerating in its moral tone, as the police would at once remove any improper character.

On the Place de la République, dominating the Place de la Rade, there stands a marble statue, by Daumas, of Charles of Anjou, who united Hyères to the crown of Provence. The houses to the right occupy the site of the Monastery of the Cordeliers, of which we have now but their ancient church remaining. This is the most complete historical monument of Hyères. It probably dates from the eighth century; and though used as a warehouse during the Revolution, it was possible to restore it completely, and this was done from 1822 to 1840. The three arched doors giving on to the place are remarkably fine; they indicate, as indeed do all portions of the church, the period of transition between the Roman and the Gothic styles of architecture, between the full-centre and the ogival or pointed arch. The interior of the church is particularly gloomy. It *The Church* *of St. Louis* is below the level of the square, and lit by small windows loaded with rich, though sombre, stained glass. These are modern imitations of ancient stained glass, by M. Marèchal, of Metz. There is a stone retable in the chapel dedicated to the Virgin, and six-reliefs by M. Fabiche, of Lyons, and a statue of the Virgin and Child by Mademoiselle de Fauveau, but the few relics of the distant past will perhaps be of more interest than these modern efforts. According to Louvet in his *Additions sur l'Histoire des troubles de Provence*, page 35, the following inscription in Latin might still be read in 1676, on a stone to the right of the main entrance :—" Here rests Sir Guillaume de Fos, Lord of Hyères, who died in the year of our Lord twelve hundred and forty. Pray for him." A similar stone to the left bore an inscription to his wife, Adélaise de Laidet. There is still distinct trace of these monuments, but the inscriptions are now illegible. Finally we should notice on either side of the high altar, two gigantic paintings, the one representing St. Louis bearing the Host, and the other the king refusing to walk under the canopy when this honour was offered to him on landing at Hyères after his return from the Crusades.

The streets of the old town wind in and out, and form a tangled maze which can scarcely be described, nor is it easy to trace a systematic itinerary through so much confusion. If, however, from the Church of St. Louis, we take the rue de la République, which passes along the top of the square, the second turning on the right will be the old rue du Cheval Blanc, and here we may note No. 29. The wood carving above the door, indicates that this house probably belonged to an order; there are a casque, a coat of arms, a bull, and horns of abundance. At the top of this street is the Oratoire, where Massillon began

The Place Massillon. his education, and which is now used as the commercial school for girls. But if we turn to our left, before reaching the school, and take the rue du Temple we shall fall into the Place Massillon, and face the Hotel de Ville and the Tower, which now constitutes the prefecture of police, but which formerly belonged to the Knights Templar. Indeed the town hall or Mairie formed part of the chapel of Saint Blaise built by the Templars, but its architectural beauties are to a great extent obliterated. The windows of the Prefecture have some ancient small stone columns ; but, the fact is, these were brought down from the convent of the Bernardine, and do not really

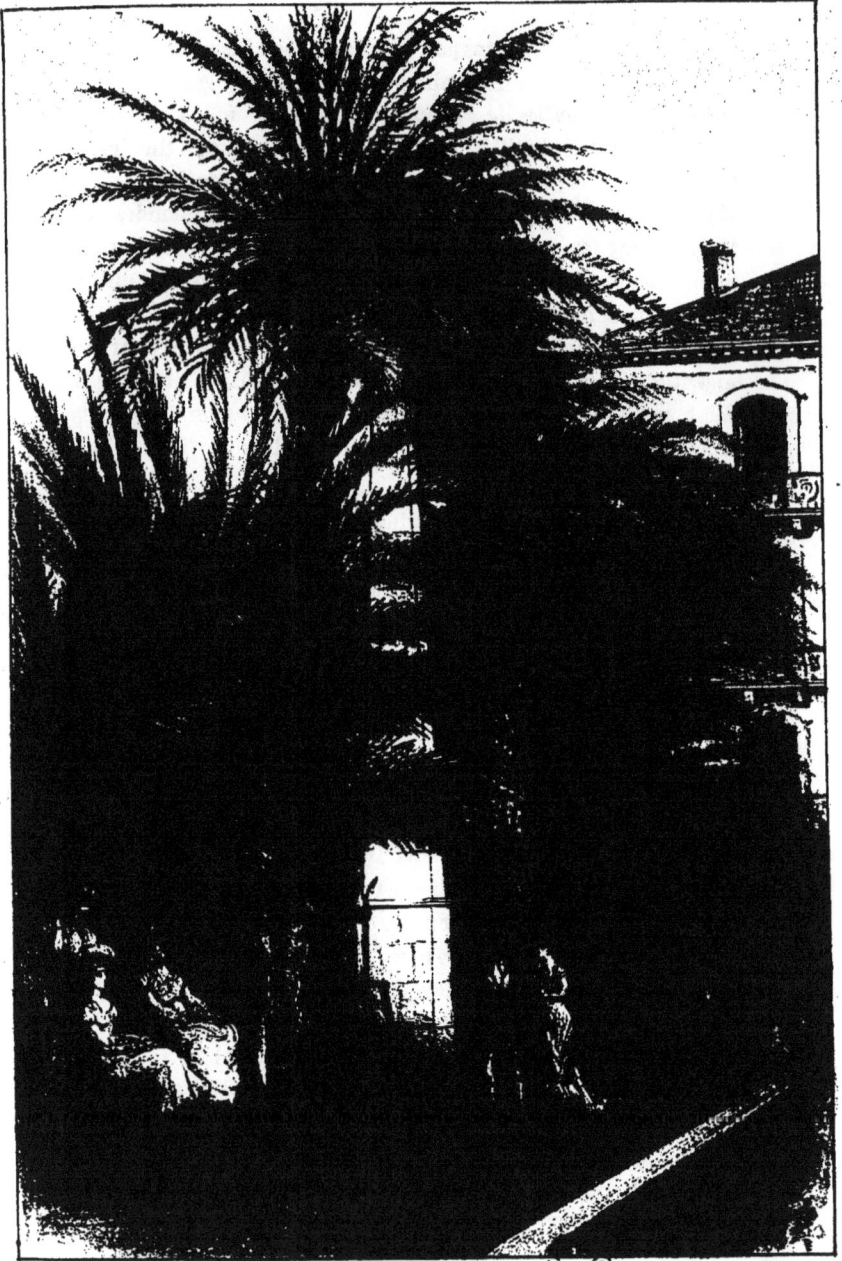

PLACE DES PALMIERS & MONUMENT.

The Garden of Hyères. Published by J. Evans & Company, 41. Bridge St. Westminster, S.W.

Copyright.

belong to this building. Inside there is another curiosity which was also brought from a distance :—a Roman Mosaic found between Cuers and the Salins on the property of M. Clapier. It is not a fine mosaic, but it is admirably preserved, and dates back to at least the second century. The nature of the design suggests that it belonged to a bath-room. The trees, the circular fish market, surrounded by the vegetable stalls, the bust of Massillon, the lofty tower of the Knights Templar, the strange winding streets, all render this place curious, picturesque and interesting. Close at hand No. 7 rue Rabaton, is the house where Massillon was born, and where there is nothing to be seen, but many bad odours that should be avoided.

Leaving the p'ace Massillon, and clambering still further up the hill, we follow the rue Ste. Catherine. Here at No. 11 is a remarkable door ; and opposite, the *The Rue Ste Catherine* ruins of the church where the bishop used to descend before the revolution to receive the *dîme*, or he tax. When other churches were not spared, it is scarcely surprising that this edifice, recalling so obnoxious an impost should have been pulled to the ground during the iconoclastic days of 1793. A little further up, the door of the Bureau de Bienfaisance, which is the French substitute to our workhouse and poor law system bears the date of 1624. Close by, at No. 8, will be found the remnants of a Roman inscription on a stone in the wall, and the date of 1572 on the door, while the house No. 17 belonged for a long time to Massillon's family.

The summit of the rue Ste. Catherine brings us to the foot of the first and most ancient city wall. The street that runs parallel is still called the Montée de Vieux Cimetiere, and yet this old cemetery was outside the town at the base of the terrace where the church of St. Paul stands. Running at angles we have the rue de la Barbacane, a term meaning a wall with loop holes, in other words the street running outside the city wall ; and this wall may be easily traced forming part of the masonry of the houses, while some of the gate-ways still remain. A little to the left is the terrace of St. Paul, where so admirable a view can be obtained. The most ancient portion of this church dates from the twelfth century. To the right is one of the old city gates, which has been recently painted blue, dotted with stars and orna-

The Hyères of Charles d'Anjou. mented with a statue of the Virgin, solely in the hope of keeping this spot clean. It was thought that these sacred effigies would inspire the inhabitants with some respect for the ancient gateway. I am assured by the proprietor who resorted to this stratagem that the manœuvre only half succeeded. Keeping to the left, we actually walk over the old city wall brought down to the level of the road and proceed to circumvent the church. This street now so deserted that it is covered with weeds, formerly led to some wealthy habitations. One house in particular must have been a very complete structure. It has still an inexhaustible well, and there are some vestiges of the ancient architecture. From here we can obtain towards the west a view of what remains of the convent of Ste. Claire. This was built close to a portion of the old wall. It consists now of a large modern white house uniting two square towers. The tower to the left was an integral part of the ancient fortifications, that to the right has been rebuilt recently, but with the old stones. This is now the property of Col. Voutier, and he caused a portion of the city wall running up behind this house to be castellated in an Oriental manner so as to recall his travels in the east. It is at the foot of this property that we find the remains of the Porte Cafabre, so named after a Captain Fabre, who commanded the militia and resisted with great heroism, the troops of Charles d'Anjou when he attacked the city of the Comtes de Fos to unite it to the dominion of the Comtes de Provence.

But, to return to the church of St. Paul, we now stand under the clock tower, where there used to be a fine door in Roman style with full centre arch, which has been walled up. To the side, the buttresses have been filled in with walls so that the fine Gothic windows are nearly concealed from the view, and can only be seen at some distance. The surrounding houses present the same incongruous appearance, modern masonry grafted on the ancient, some of the doors bearing dates of the sixteenth century. From behind the church, *Old Houses* the rue St. Bernard slants in a northerly direction up the hill, and we notice at once at No. 2 remains of a fine house. The small portion of the wall still standing indicates the formation of a magnificent Roman window, and there are persons still living who remember admiring it in its entirety. Opposite this ruin there is a smaller door leading out of the fortifications, and a handsome Gothic window now closed in.

Making a digression to the left we go a few steps along the rue Ste. Claire and note a bold lofty Gothic arch, now half walled up, but still retaining all the gracefulness of its outline. The house No. 8 belonged in 1780 to Mr Guy de St. Tropoz and had a window, of which there still remain distinct traces, dating evidently from the period of the crusades. The stone work had the form of a cross, but this has all been walled in, and modern windows, built amidst these ancient traces of art and wealth. In the middle ages this street was inhabited by the goldsmiths of the town, it was the Cheapside of Hyères, and yet now it looks a poverty stricken collection of old and modern dilapitated houses. No. 10 was, however, an exception, for here a bishop resided. The episcopal keys are still engraved on the old stone work of the door. From this point also a good view can be obtained of the Gothic windows of St. Paul. In the neighbouring rue du Four another clerical house will be found with a fine arched door which has been recently injured.

Returning to the rue St. Bernard we reach at its summit the end of the houses of the old town. Here are terraces on which olive and almond trees, peas, beans, and other vegetables grow, where houses, and churches and convents once stood. Here stood, to the left, the church of St. Pierre and, in front, the convent to the Bernardines, both sacked and destroyed during the great revolution. It is impossible even now not o admire *The Bernar- dine.* the site of the convent commanding an admirable view, wonderfully sheltered from the cold winds, and possessing a terrace where each sister had a little garden well exposed to the sun. These sisters were all younger daughters of the nobility who formed a community here, and lived cheaply and most comfortably without touching the large fortunes of the eldest child, and thus weakening the privileges of primogeniture. At the revolution, however, this sisterhood was scattered and many of its members married the inhabitants of Hyères and became useful mothers and housewives. The ancient porte de Pierrefeu, now called la Souquette, stood where the wall that goes up to the dungeon and castle meets the road. By descending the rue St. Bernard again for a short distance and then taking to the left the rue du Roche, er the Montée St. Bernard, we come to the rue du Paradis and the Porte Barue. The latter is wonderfully preserved and imposing with its double portals, the grooves for the two sliding doors, and the hinges for the ordinary dore or gate, used in times of peace. Outside this gate, is the Barbacane, and inside running parallel and both leading us back to St. Paul is the rue du Paradis. Here in a corner house opposite No. 12 will be found a stone in the wall bearing the remains of a Latin inscription and fine small marble columns partially covered with masonry may still be seen in the windows.

It will be easy to understand after this walk that the ancient town of Hyères, the town of the Comtes de Fos of Charles d'Anjou and St. Louis extended where the walls now still exist by the Porte de Pierrefeu right round the rock and castle to the north-west and then down the hill past the monastery of Ste. Claire to the porte Cafavre. From here the ancient wall cut through *The first Wall.* what is now the heart of the old town passing by the church of St. Paul, where there is the old gate, then along the Barbacane to the Porte Barue and round the Bernardines back to the Porte de Pierrefeu. Afterwards a second town was built extending from the Bernardines to

THE AVENUE OF PALMS, WITH ENGLISH CHURCH.

Copyright.

the corner of the avenue du Repos, where an old tower may be seen along the Place Strasbourg to the Porte des Salins on the place de la Rade. Hence the wall, as already stated, skirts the Route Nationale till it reaches the place des Palmiers, and then goes up the hill again and joins the older wall at the Porte Cafabre.

The castle itself is, however, more attractive than these old streets and this old town. It has the advantage of standing in the open, away from insalubrious odours, of commanding a magnificent landscape, and of being covered with wild flowers, shrubs, and trees. Near the site of the old Porte Pierrefeu, there is a high stone wall with a green door with a bell attached that rings on opening. The peasant farmers who cultivate the land round the ruins live within, and may expect a small gratuity if they render the visitor any assistance. It happens sometimes, however, when the solitary inhabitant of the rock is away that the door is locked. On these occasions, the more adven- *Entrance* turous make bold to climb over a low wall a little *Castle.* distance to the left of the door. This is strictly illegal, as the castle and surrounding grounds, are private property, but nevertheless, no one is likely to object to such tresspass. From the Place des Palmiers a winding road leads to this point, passing by the Russian Consulate, up the Montée Ste. Claire, and the rue St. Bernard. Or else, from the Place de Strasbourg we can follow the rue Neuf or the rue du Bourg Neuf up to the Bernardines, and thence find the green door which is the only available entrance to the castle grounds.

Interesting as the exploration of these grounds must seem to all who visit them, both on account of the magnificent views that stretch out for miles around, and of the vegetation and the ruins we tread under foot, there is not much more to add to the description of the Chateau than what will be found in the chapter on the History of Hyères. It is when we bear this history in mind, when we recall the sieges that this castle has withstood, and the important part it played when it sided against the town that lies at its feet, during the religious wars in the time of Henri IV that the interest of the visit to the old ruins is really developed, and enhances the enjoyment of the magnificent scenery which has feebly but frequently been described.

After passing the farmer's cottage near the entrance gate a winding path takes us towards the northerly extremity of the old wall and not far from one of the square towers. These, however, can be reached more easily from a higher point, and should be visited, as here will be found some of the masonry already mentioned, and which seems to indicate that they were built in the fifth or sixth century. The path winds *The Castle grounds.* in and out through terraces where the gay almond blossom blends with the "mysterious green]" of the olive tree, the practical potato growing at their feet. As we near the summit we pass a small opening on a level with the ground, and below there is an underground passage that would invite exploration, but for the absence of the lamps and ladders. Now a terrace is reached guarded by a magnificent cypress that stands erect and majestic like a giant sentinel watching over the inland valley of the Sauvette, and the rampart and the three towers at his feet. The cemetery lies silently beyond, the white tomb stones harmonising in their record of wrecked hopes with the grey crumbling walls that once proudly upheld the glory and power of the castle and its lord.

The entrance of the castle is well preserved, though aloes, wall flowers, and other plants have found earth enough to grow from between almost every crevice in the walls. We can still note how cunningly the approaches were defended, and the alliance of nature with art, represented by a huge rock *The Old Walls.* that towers above and formed part of the wall, must have produced an appalling effect on the assailants. To the right, as we pass the gate the stone bearing the inscription *nobile castrum arcearum* shows that the castle existed before the eleventh century ; and it is indeed very certain that, at all times, this high summit was inhabited, and used as a place of defence. Here the Romans established an *oppidum*, and Dr J. B. Jaubert points out in his work on pre-historic Hyères, that in the most inaccessible recesses on the north-west side of the rock there are several portions of walls which are undoubtedly of Celtic origin, and probably more than two thousand years old !

A variety of paths tempt us, when once we are in the castle, and they should one and all be explored. These twist in and out between a combination of masonry and rocks, with dark romantic recesses, leading suddenly to small natural, or artificial terraces that command views so vast that it seems as if the fairest portion of the world lay at *The View.* our feet. From the summit, we can see to the other side of the mountain, and here the Fenouillet, the Faron, and the Coudon lift their points high into the sky. There are glimpses of the sea that rolls near Toulon, the fertile plain of la Garde stretches for miles before us, while the entire pine clad range of the mountains des Oiseaux seems close at hand. When we turn round, the endless mountains of the Maure range meets our gaze, while close at hand old towers, masonry, crumbling steps, tottering walls, loop-holes that still seem to frown on some imaginary enemy, invite our inspection.

On the highest point, there is a miserable little round towers of evident modern and shoddy construction which is fortunately falling to pieces, and near to it the iron cross *An Original* and two marble tomb stones mark the place *Resting* *Place.* where the late proprietor of this rock and his his wife are buried. In selecting this place of interment, they certainly displayed an originality of character and a worthy affection for an interesting spot ; and if their personal qualities were at all in keeping with the eulogistic epitaphs that will be read on these tomb-stones, the rock that held Charles of Anjou in defiance, was never owned by worthier proprietors.

In conclusion, we should observe that the ascent to the castle commences in the town itself, the winding nature of the path renders the walk less arduous, the many stones and seats will enable delicate persons to rest on the road, and as the highest point to be reached is only 670 feet above the sea, it may be attempted even by some invalids !

ROUND AND ABOUT HYÈRES ON FOOT.

CHAPTER VII.

The exceptional number and charms of the walks and excursions near Hyères constitute the principal source of enjoyment available to those who are able to appreciate fine scenery, or who are interested in natural history. These expeditions may be prolonged to a great distance, and yet there are panoramas of incomparable beauty that unroll themselves at our feet while still within the walls of the town itself. On the hill side, from the centre of the old town, from the terrace of the church of St. Paul, the plain, the anchorage, and the island of Hyères stretch out for miles and miles in the clear atmosphere, sparkle in the sunlight, and offer to the gaze endless variety of colour and landscape. This view, beautiful in itself, is extended, and its charms intensified, as we ascend; but, without any great exertion, a wonderful choice of scenes may be visited, and all within easy walking distance even for an invalid.

The stranger is at liberty to stroll in every direction; he may trespass *ad libitum* as long as he shows common consideration for the interests of the persons on whose grounds he uninvited treads. The fields, the terraces on the hill sides are generally kept in a high state of cultivation, sown with early vegetables, green peas, broad beans, artichokes, and a number of other *primeurs* with which Hyères supplies the North during the arid winter months. Care must, therefore be taken not to injure these tender plants, *Trespassing* and this can generally be done by skirting along the edge of the fields. If the peasant or proprietor happens to be out at work in his grounds, a salutation with the hand or cap, a friendly *bonjour* in passing, will be a sufficient acknowledgement and apology for the intrusion. Indeed, it is surprising how far a little civility will go in France. Of course, mere civility will scarcely cover an injury done, and the politest of bows will barely atone for picking almond or other blossoms from fruit bearing trees; but, so long as the stranger is affable and courteous, no attempt will be made to restrict his enjoyment. Thus we may freely saunter through field and woodland, nor need any fear be entertained of losing the road. For sign-posts there are the eternal hills which can be seen from all points, indicating the way home. To the north-east the Maures mountains seem rolling over each other like huge green billows. To the west, the cone-like point of the Fenouillet is a nearer landmark. The craggy, bare Faron, with its huge nose-shaped peak, rising on the horizon; while half-way between it and the Fenouillet the Coudon may be likened to Napoleon

Nature's Signposts. lying in state. The head seems to have sunk in the pillow, but the nose and chin stand forth with characteristic decisiveness, the the body slants downwards, and the feet rise out as if from under a sheet or shroud, at the extreme end of the mountain ridge. To the south again, there are the Ermitage, the pine-clad hill of Costebelle, and the small green range of the Montagne des oiseaux, with the fortified summit of the Col Noir appearing between it and the more easterly Montagne du Paradis, which vaguely recalls in its outline the Egyptian sphinx. Finally, as if this were not sufficient to guide our footsteps, there are the hill and castellated rock of Hyères itself, which may be seen from every prominent point for miles around. Once the configuration of these four ranges of mountains and their respective positions are understood, a matter of five minutes' study to anyone who possesses the bump of locality, there is no longer any danger of losing the way.

Within a short distance of the town there are many interesting walks, which are more easily discovered than described. They offer no special historical interest, but it would be difficult to find anything more lovely so near home. For instance, taking a north-easterly direction, we arrive by the Boulevart de l'Orient, after passing a high embankment bristling with aloes, to the extensive private gardens of the villa Chateaubriand, which are generally thrown open to the public. If, on the contrary, a more northerly direction is taken, an avenue leading past the cemetery, and appropriately called l'Avenue du Repos, brings us to the hills that form part of the Maurettes, and lie immediately behind the rock of Hyères. Here we may *Round the Castle Hill.* saunter about indefinitely amid pine and cork trees, with the lenticus, the juniper, the Mediterranean heath reaching breast high, while at our feet hundreds of wild flowers cluster round. Then, bearing in a westerly direction, we pass behind the mountain that shelters Hyères, and through olive groves and vineyards, regain the town at its western extremity after having described a circle which will have afforded many opportunities for landscape painting, and not necessitated an ascension of more than five hundred feet.

If, however, a longer walk is desired, then a direct northerly course may be followed till the small range of the Maurettes has been crossed, and the broad, flat plain, known as La Bravette, or the Vallon du Muat, is reached, and here, to the north-east, the Gapeau, the largest river in the neighbourhood, will be found. On this side of the hills the scenery loses in a great measure its Southern aspect, and recalls the English country. Yet this general impression is soon dispelled by the examination of details. The course of the Gapeau is marked by a double wall of luxur- *The Gapeau* ious trees that grow on either side, drawing nutriment from its parched banks, which, at the rare intervals of rain, scarcely suffice to keep in control the raging torrent, though in fine weather it seems but as a rivulet.

High up these trees and forming a thick veil of greenery the false sarsaparilla clings with its bright, spade-like leaves, on branch and twig and trunk, and seems like a barrier placed by nature to protect, to shade, and hide the precious water that rolls past below. This is a favourite spot for picnics; and by following the river, the high road from Hyères to St. Tropez is reached, so that the latter part of the journey may be performed on smooth if dusty ground.

Before, however, taking this walk, the visitor will, in all probability, have made his pilgrimage to the Ermitage. Stories of the marvellous escapes attributed to the intercession of the Virgin for those who have addressed prayers to her from this spot will assuredly have been related to him; for it is easy to discern that the people of Provence are more ignorant, and therefore more superstitious than the inhabitants of the North. For instance, I heard the landlady of an hotel at Hyères, whose husband's life is supposed to have been saved in recognition for his devotions at the Ermitage, solemnly give the following advice: The gentleman to whom she was speaking was very anxious about his little boy, who was seriously ill, presumably from the effects of a sun-stroke. The land-

Popular Supersti-tions.

lady, however, protested that there was no danger whatsoever in this, the sunstroke could be cured in a few hours. It was only necessary to be up early in the morning, to watch from the window in the direction of the Ermitage till the church was lit by the glow of the rising sun; then if a cross was made on the child's forehead, and a special prayer uttered at the precise moment when the sun first appeared, a certain and almost instantaneous cure would ensue. The landlady insisted that she had tried this method on her own children with the greatest success, and pro-tested that she would never think of calling in a doctor or wasting her money on medicines for a case of sun-stroke when a costless and far more effective remedy was so easily obtained.

Under such circumstances, the peculiar, not to say comic,

character of some of the numerous pictures that hang on the walls of the Ermitage church will scarcely surprise the visitor. The tall steeple surmounted by a massive statue of the Virgin can be seen from almost every window in Hyères that has a southern aspect, and, as there are sign-posts on the road when the church itself cannot be seen, there is no difficulty in reaching this point. A portion of the plain *The Plain* must be crossed, and then a gentle ascent of the Montague des Oiseaux is made. The Ermitage is on a summit, at an elevation of 321 feet. It is a heavy structure, with Roman pillars, an ogival roof and a modern steeple. In fact, it is scarcely calculated to elicit the admiration of a purist. On the other hand, the view to be obtained from the terrace on which the church stands is most remarkable. This is an excellent point from which to appreciate the topographical situation of Hyères, as it lies some three miles distant on the other side of the plain. The exposed position of the English quarter, the sheltered nook in which the old town nestles, can be appreciated at a glance. Then we can note how marvellously flat is the plain which has been redeemed from the sea, and where St. Louis sailed up to the walls of Hyères in the ships that bore him home from Palestine. To the east of the plain, Les Salins with their parks of shallow blue water stretching inland, evaporating under the hot rays of the sun, suggest that with very little provocation, the sea might be persuaded to rush in again between the mountains, and thus at one fell swoop rob Paris of its early vegetable supply.

A guardian lives in a house that seems to form part of the church, and will, on the ringing of a bell, open the church to visitors. The first objects that attract attention on entering are two huge flags suspended over the aisles. The one was brought home from the Crusades, and the other is an English Union Jack, taken from an English ship by a French privateer manned probably by men in part recruited at Hyères. Then high on the walls hang innumerable trophies; the hats of sailors saved from drowning, the swords of officers spared in action, the iron fetters of criminals released before the expiration of their sentence, guns that have burst without hurting their owners, the nosegay which a youth held in his hand when con- confirmed in his bed after all hope had been abandoned, and who, nevertheless, recovered from his dangerous illness, the crutches of the lame who regained the use of their limbs, and many other tokens. Yet, in spite of all the miracles performed by Notre Dame des Oiseaux, the church itself was not saved from the effects of time or the assaults of war. Two cannon balls may be noted firmly implanted in its walls; while the stations of the cross, where the faithful worshipped as they crawled on their knees from the bottom to the summit of the hill, have fallen into ruins. One was swept away by the railway, and no one has cared to replace it, others fell to pieces naturally, while those still standing have been robbed of their pictures by the force of the mistral.

The Ermitage trophies

Inside the church, pictures still abound and are to be numbered by the hundred. They are all supposed to illustrate marvellous escapes due to the personal intercession of Notre Dame des Oiseaux. Some of these are ancient; thus there is a picture of a sick man in bed bearing the date of 1612, and another of 1613. A woman is spared by the thunder, which enters by the window and goes out by the chimney. This picture is dated 1791, and we must confess that the strange course followed by the thunder-bolt is not very accurately rendered. The most interesting picture is that, however, which represents the brother of the great Massillon, whose gun burst while shooting wild ducks on the 2nd of December, 1773, and who, it is confidently asserted, owed his life solely to his devotion to this shrine. Among the more modern pictures, a great many relate to escapes at sea. There is a sailor falling from a mast, a boat upset in a squall, a ship set on fire, and similar incidents. The narrow escapes on land are, however, more original. Apart from a plethora of gun explosions, which does not speak well for the local gunsmiths, and of persons run over by carts, a result *Illustrated Miracles.* not complimentary to local driving, we have a scene of a mad dog in a kitchen, a mason who contrives to fall through five stories of a house, a cask having fallen first to make a convenient hole for him through each of the five floors; a woman falls out of a window while a man jumps off a balcony to save her; then an infuriated mule is gnawing at the arm of his master, two women descending the St Baune are overtaken by a gigantic avalanche, a carriage full of people is shot over the bridge of the Gapeau, and in another painting the Gapeau itself has broken loose and overtakes several persons, and yet, in all these cases no one was drowned, nor hurt, nor bit, and in fact none the worse for the dangers to which they were exposed. Most of these pictures are abominably painted, the gratitude of the devotees was evidently not equal to disbursing a fee likely to secure the services of a competent artist. Yet there is one picture a little better than the rest. It represents one of the narrow streets of the old town of Hyères, where a child fell from a third floor window and was not hurt. Dr. Vidal, it is stated, was at once called to see the child, and will vouch for the accuracy of this fact; but I have yet to learn that this eminent practitioner or any one else can trace the connection between the votive chapel and the escape experienced by the child. Indeed, it has been suggested that an opposition chapel might appropriately be built where trophies and pictures of all persons who have not escaped from some special danger might be hung; and it is further urged that this new collection would soon become the more numerous of the two. In the meanwhile, the Ermitage is well worth a visit, particularly on the 25th of March, when the annual pilgrimage takes place, and hundreds of persons arrive from great distances to offer prayers at this shrine and to picnic under the surrounding pine trees.

If the distance (about three miles) be considered too great the Ermitage may be reached with much less exertion. The omnibus can be taken to the railway station, and thus more than half the distance is accomplished for a mere trivial outlay. If this does not suffice, by waiting at the station till the train comes in a seat may be secured in the omnibus from the Hotel et Pension de l'Ermitage, and this vehicle passes within two or three hundred yards of the chapel. A similar stratagem will bring the visitor back to Hyères with equal facility and economy.

The direction of the Ermitage may also be taken for two or three other pleasant excursions. After crossing the railway line by the road a little to the right of the station, a little chapel, — or "station of the cross" will be reached, where three roads branch off in different directions. A poster indicates that the central road leads to the Pension de l'Ermitage, where so many English persons reside and enjoy the beautiful surrounding scenery and the healthy perfume of the pine trees. It is easy to see that the road to the left goes in a direct line to the church of the Ermitage, while the road to the right is perhaps *The road to the the easiest means of reaching the Grotte Grotto.* des Fées. After passing a few villas well sheltered on the side of a small hill, the road brings us to a large quarry dug at the base of two hills. Crossing the quarry and passing a small cottage on the other side we turn to the right and ascend to the summit of the small hill, and here will be found the Grotte des Fées. The entrance is a small hole not a yard square in size, with an iron rail trap over it, which has to be lifted up to admit the visitor. Looking towards the sea, it will be seen that the grotto faces the cleft between the smaller and the larger Montagne des Oiseaux, the quarry and the Ermitage will then be to our left, the summit of the hill on which we stand is bare and the entrance to the grotto is a hole like that of a well between a few small rocks.

CHURCH OF THE ERMITAGE.

Copyright.

ANCIENT GATEWAY IN OLD TOWN.

The Garden of Hyères. Published by J. Evans & Company, 11. Bridge St Westminster. S.W.

To visit this place in safety, a party of three or four should go together, well provided with matches and candles. The entrance is very small and it is necessary to crawl on all fours. Thus we reach several large apartments of the most weird appearance where the crystalized limestone sparkles over dark holes and forbidding crevices. A false step might result in a dangerous fall, and if the single light of a solitary visitor were extinguished and dropped in the fall, it would be almost impossible to find the way out. Hence there should be several persons together, each armed with candles. With this ordinary precaution the visit will be most interesting and the descent into the centre of the mountain romantic and curious. The closeness and the heat of the grotto may, however, be found inconvenient, and a wrap on coming out will be a welcome precaution. It has already been mentioned, that a special blind insect, unknown elsewhere, lives in this grotto. It belongs to the *carabas* genus, but is much smaller, and is called the *Anophtalma Raymondi*. Thoughts of fairies, of more probable brigands and smugglers, of the Cacoterie and Bageauderie of past ages, will occur to those who visit this hiding place provided by the laws of nature to conceal the wretched fugitives who have sinned against the laws of man.

The Fairy's Grotto.

From the grotto, Hyères may be reached without returning to the Costebelle road, but by taking paths across the Quartier des Loubes, which is the name given to that portion of the plain that may be seen from the hill lying between the grotto and the town of Hyères.

Before concluding this account of the short walks to be taken, I should not omit to mention the Plage or sea beach of the Ceinturon. This portion of the coast is approached by train; La Plage is the next station after Hyères. The distance is about three miles, and is, therefore, within walking distance; or, finally, an omnibus can be taken to the station and the rest of road about half the distance done on foot. In summer an omnibus from Hyères to the Plage takes bathers down to the waters' edge. At present, the accom-modation is very scarce and there are no means of obtaining even the most modest form of refreshment. A few pretty, but somewhat isolated villas line a portion of the beach; a wood of magnificent umbrella pines occupies the rest of the ground and affords shelter within a stone's throw of the sea. The race course is also close at hand, and there are the marshes where wild fowl may be shot. Frogs of various species and the beautiful green lizard, the *Oselata*, which measures a foot in length, will be found in abundance in some stagnant water between the wood that separates the race course from the beach, and the first of the row of villas. The sight of these brilliant animals running like rats to take refuge in the embankments suggests a semi-tropical region, but the cool sea breeze will create an appetite that recalls the more bracing climates of the North.

The Sea Beach.

CHAPTER VIII.

There is no limit to the number of excursions that can be made with good horses and a light carriage within driving distance of Hyères. Not only are there many points that should be visited, but these can be reached by many roads so that the same place may be re-visited several times without going over the same ground. The drive round the range of mountains to the south-west of the town is generally the first that suggests itself, particularly as it embraces the ruins of Pomponiana, the village and sea-beach of Carqueyranne. The best road is that of the Almanarre, then right round the entire range of moun- tains back to Hyères by the Toulon road, but this is, perhaps, the least interesting and certainly runs over the most level ground. Then again Pomponiana can be reached by the Costèbelle road which enables us to pass close to St. Pierre les Horts, that remarkable mansion built with platforms, dungeon, drawbridge, and castellated towers—recalling the castle of a feudal baron still armed and prepared to resist the aggression of the Moors. The style of architecture dates from the time of Philip Augustus, but as this eccentric dwelling was in reality built only a few years ago it contains all the modern appliances and comforts known in these days of comparative civilization. The construction is well calculated to revive the souvenirs which the district calls to the mind. Close at hand the fragments of Notre Dame de Lorette, *St. Pierre* and not far distant to the immediate east of the Castrum of Pomponiana, the ruins of St. Pierre de de l'Almanarre, show what the Moors did, and how necessary it was to fortify the district. There is a long and romantic history attached to the institution of St. Pierre de l'Almanarre. It was first a monastery where the monks behaved in so scandalous a manner that the Pope Honorius III. had to interfere; then three centuries later, St. Pierre became a convent, and the sisters seem also to have behaved in a very light manner. At last the pretty abbess, the daughter of one of the noblest houses of Provence, doubting the devotion of the inhabitants of Hyères, caused the alarm bell to be rang in the middle of the night to see whether in the event of an attack, they would as they had promised come armed to defend the convent. The citizens, however, kept their word, and soon a small army was down on the coast seeking the enemy. Naturally the gallant defenders were not a little irritated at the false cry of wolf and the doubt it implied of their courage and fidelity. As in the fable, the sequence was soon at hand. Shortly after this event, the Moors came in real earnest, but it was now in vain that the abbess rang the alarm-bell. From Hyères no one moved, the Moors sacked the convent, and only seven sisters escaped from their clutches. Such is the history of the ruin that stands close to the Castrum of Pomponiana.

The road of Almanarre reaches the sea just at the point of the angle formed by the narrow strip of sand that unites what was the island of Giens to the mainland and the beach. The name is evidently derived from the Moorish term *Al Manar*, lighthouse or signal, and it is here that the Romans built a pier jutting out into the sea, to facilitate the landing from boats at a time when Giens being an island there was nothing to prevent the sea dashing in from the East. The ruins of this pier are still distinctly traced, and close at hand will be found some very perfect baths. Even the paint remains on a portion of the walls and the steps down to what was the water,—and is now nothing but mud and refuse. On the inland side of the road, beyond a vineyard, and in a cluster of pine trees, will be found

the ruins of the Roman *Castrum.* All the walls and masonry
have been thrown over in the same direction
by an earthquake which occurred in the sixth *Pompon-iana and the Roman Bathes.*
century; but it is easy to trace the Roman masonry,
the Roman bricks at regular intervals between
the stones, and the peculiar square shape given to the stones
used for the outer portion of the walls. In the centre will still
e found the well, now filled up with stones, and in a field close by
a more modern well with a Roman stone tomb used as a trough!
Here it was that Prince Frederick of Denmark organized
systematic researches and that a number of interesting Roman
relics have been found. Even now broken pieces of Roman
pottery can be picked up on all sides. All this has led to the
supposition that the bright and happy Roman town called
Olbia by Strabon was situated on this site, but the fact is that,
though Olbia undoubtedly existed somewhere in the neighbourhood of Hyères, no one knows the precise position of this town.
The result is that Olbia has awakened more interest, occasioned
more disputes, and has been more talked about now that it has
ceased to exist, than in the times of its greatest prosperity,
Even the band at Hyères has been entitled the "Lyre of
Olbia."

Close to the old Roman baths there are some modern bathing
establishments which are equally worthy of notice, though from
a totally different point of view. These consist of little wooden
huts built along the beach and generally carefully closed.
They belong to the workmen, peasants and gardeners of the
district who have clubbed together to defray in common the
cost of these simple little structures. They
pay a small sum to the municipality for the *Co-operative Baths.*
use of the few yards of land these modest
cabins occupy, and thus secure a little seaside resort.
On summer days and holidays these prudent toilers come
to Pomponiana, and, undressing in their wooden huts, enjoy
baths on the same coast where formerly the luxurious Roman

besported himself. After a swim, a bouillabaise is concocted, with a song for dessert and jokes to enliven the road home. This assuredly is a refined and healthy means of enjoyment, and it does great credit to the tastes of the industrial classes of Hyères.

From Pomponiana, the road turns in a westerly direction, and, skirting the sea, passes San Salvador, where a magnificent mansion is in course of construction. It is nominally built for M. Magnier, the proprietor of the " Evenement," but a halo of
San Solvador
mystery overhangs its real destiny. It is, however, a most handsome mansion, though the estate is surrounded by ugly walls that spoil the scenery and which no one with any sense of art or any public spirit would ever have constructed. Here will be found the palm tree which was removed at so great a cost and with so much difficulty from Dr Vidal's garden at Hyères.

A little further, and we pass by a cluster of umbrella pines leaning over the sea, and approach a little restaurant where, in what was the chapel of St. Vincent, a fairly good *bouillabaise* and breakfast may be enjoyed for a moderate outlay. It would be more prudent, however, to send notice on the previous evening if a good *déjeuner* is required. In the village itself of Carqueyranne, there is another little restaurant also close to the shore, and on the road to the first battery which commands the anchorage of Giens. At the second battery, a couple or three miles further on the coast, will be found the copper mines which
Carqeyranne.
are well worth a visit. Formerly, from this point it was usual to ascend the Col Noir, from whence one of the finest views in the neighbourhood could be obtained. But now this summit has lost its dark pine trees, a fortress has been built there, and the foreigner who might venture to climb up this hill would run a serious risk of being arrested as a Prussian spy. The whole of the district, from Carqueyranne to Pomponiana, is

remarkable for its magnificent scenery, but also for the warmth of its climate, this is, on an average two to three degrees Farhenheit warmer than Hyères, and yet rendered supportable by the fresh sea breeze. The vegetation here is perhaps a fort-night in advance of that of Hyères, and the protection afforded from the mistral, the dreaded icy north-west wind, is as com-plete as mountains can make it. On the other hand, the district lies close to the sea and suffers from all the inconveniences that arise from proximity to the Mediterranean. By far the pleasantest way to reach Carqueyranne, is to persuade the coachman to adventure himself over the hills by way of the Vallon. A rough road leads through the mountains, passing over the dip between the Montague du Paradis and the Montague des Oiseaux. The more able-bodied members of the expedition will have to leave the carriage and walk when the steepest point is reached, but the view of Hyères and the Maures to the north-east, and of the sea to the south, will be an ample reward for this small effort. With donkeys all the sur-rounding mountains are accessible, and innumerable pleasant expeditions may be made under the shade and amid the scent of the pine trees.

The Montagne du Paradis is difficult, or at least tiring to climb, but like its neighbours the summit affords an excellent view. Many persons will, however, prefer loitering in the picturesque and rambling village of Carquey-ranne which had at least the advantage of _The Sea Shore._ eliciting the admiration of Augustin Thierry the celebrated historian who consequently lived here for for several years. The shores also, with their rocks, sand, shells, seaweeds loaded with minute particles of coral, with cuttle fish, an occasional spunge, and other curiosities tempt the idler. Children will delight in the felt-like balls which the sea manufactures by rolling together fragments of sea-weed, and that abound on the whole line of coast.

Having thus explored the coast and the hills to the south, the visitor will find that there is another most agreeable drive round the Maurettes, a chain of hills to the north of Hyères. Following the Toulon road for a little distance, the carriage then branches off to the right, and working round the base of the Fenouillet, passes by the rich gardens on the banks of the Beal where Jean and Pierre Natte built now nearly four

The Jean Natte canal. centuries ago, the first canal hat brought water to Hyères. This canal is still in existence and still of great use to the town, which it reaches just opposite the Hotel des Iles d'Or; it then follows the Boulevart National, passes under the Place des Palmiers, and, turning at angles near the Porte Portalet, supplies the water for the public wash-houses near the Jardin

La Crau, Sauvebonne, and Pierre-feu. Huber. The aqueduct near La Crau is a remarkable specimen of the hydraulic architecture of the fifteenth century. From the prosperous village of La Crau, with its handsome plane tree walk, its prim new church, the road to the north-east leads to the Vallée de Sauvebonne where formerly the land was farmed by the Knight Templars and which is still one of the richest, and most productive corners of the Garden of Hyères. Now only a few fragments remain of the Templar's dwelling place which had been built with all the art and refinement known in the middle ages. To the north overlooking the little rivulet, the Beal, there is the convent of the Toulon Marists, and much farther on, but too far, perhaps, for the one day's excursion, is the village of Pierrefeu where Madame de Sault d'Agoult held her famous classes when she taught the arts of love to the troubadours of Provence and heard them rehearse their songs and poems. From the culminating point of this site a magnificent view is obtained.

The road home brings us to the banks of the Gapeau which must be followed till the road from Hyères to St. Tropez has been reached. Within the vast circle thus visited smaller circles can be made, including other points of interest. From La Crau the commencement of Jean Natte's aqueduct may be visited at La Castile, and then the carriage might return by La Roquette, thus keeping closer to the Maurettes range. By this road, the banks of the Gapeau are reached at an earlier stage, and the freshness and verdure they engender thus enjoyed at greater length. Within this circle is the mountain of the Fenouillet; a most agreeable ascension. *The Fenouillet.* The distance is about four miles from the town, but allowance must be made for the climbing. The best road for donkeys and pedestrians is the path that passes behind the castle of Hyères and is reached from the porte de la Sauvette. Keeping generally to the left, the path skirts along the summit of the minor hills and then winds up the peak of the Fenouillet, at the base of which a little chapel will be found on the side opposite to Hyères and over-looking La Crau. From the summit of the elevation or peak, and when standing by the side of a huge white cross the entire surrounding country can be seen;—Toulon and its anchorage, the Point of Six-Fours, where the Romans pitched their camp, the whole course of the Gapeau, the Maures, the sea, Hyères, its plain and its islands. The rough climb up the rock that crowns this mountain is further rewarded by a glass of Fenouillet, a sort of Chartreuse made from the herbs that grow on the mountain, and from which it derives its name (*fœniculum*, fine herb). Some slight remains of masonry suggests that this point was fortified in remote ages, and the archiologist will find here subjects for study.

The excursions to the east of Hyères are, with the exception of Les Salins, more lengthy. The Salins may either be visited by the smooth route de St. Tropez, the great high-road, or by the rougher chemin du Père Eternal. This latter road passes over the water supply of the town which is pumped from this point to the reservoir at the summit of the Montagne du Paradis by a fifty horse power engine. When the Gapeau is reached, it must be crossed at a ford; but, in ordinary weather, the water does not reach the spokes of the carriage wheels, and there is some charm in crossing the river in this primitive manner. On the other hand, tLe St. Tropez road takes us over a bridge with a pointed arch dating probably from the fourteenth century. The Salins are also surrounded by the halo of antiquity. There is still a document extant which proves that the Salins were made over to the Abbey of St. Victor in 1072, and they doubtless existed long before this date. The importance of these salt marshes may also be gathered from the fact that in 1325 the proprietors gave 160,000 pots or measures of salt to redeem the Castle of Bréganson which protects the anchorage in front of the Salins. These salt marshes have naturally been the property of a great variety of owners, and on one or two occasions fell into the hands of the church which they helped to enrich. In 1856, they were purchased by the Compagnie Parisienne des Salins du Midi, and under M. Laurent's management extended over a thousand acres; these produce annually about 20,000 tons of 1000 kilogrammes each, which are sold at 10 to 12 francs per ton, thus yielding an income of about £10,000. Sixty workmen are permanently employed and about three hundred when the water, being evaporated and the saline particles crystalized, the time has arrived for gathering the harvest.

The Salins

From Les Salins we may push a point further to Les Bormettes, the delightful villa built by Horace Vernet, and where there is still one of his unfinished paintings representing his game-keeper killing a fox. The likeness is all the more striking as the game-keeper is well known in the neighbourhood. The present proprietor of this ideal residence devotes his energy not to painting but to horticulture; and the grounds surrounding his chateau are richly studded with the rarest specimens. There are no less than thirty-four different sorts of Australian acacias, notably *Mimosa Hudsonii* and the *Mimosa Dammar*, from

Les Bormettes.

whence the gum d'amar is taken. The *Protea argenta* is the finest or rarest tree in the garden, with its leaves of silvered velvet. There are also a number of remarkable *Grevillea*, the *longifolia* with its saw-like leaves, and the *rupestris* with its red pine shaped branch. The *Calothamnus Sanguineas*, is particularly curious, its red flower growing out of a little grey pod that has the ears and the tail, the colour and appearance of a little mouse.

Beyond Les Bormettes, we pass the little stream and estate of Le Pellegrin, where the present owner, Dr Vidal, is making bold and worthy efforts to stamp out the phyloxera. We have now fairly left the plain and are once more engaged amid mountains covered with pine and cork oak and all the remarkable plants and wild flowers *Le Pellegrin.* that are the glory of this country. Here and there on the coasts are secluded, small, but delightful beaches, well sheltered by rocks and mountains where the discreet bather may undisturbed enjoy a plunge in the blue waters. On this estate also, there is a small hill covered with the remnants of tombs, and innumerable specimens of Roman, Gallo Roman, and pure Celtic brick may be gathered in abundance.

From the Pellegrin, and after crossing the stream that gives its name to the estate, a road will be reached which runs from the main highway to St. Tropez, and leads to the Chateau de Léoube and the Chateau de Bréganson. From Hyères to Breganson the entire journey may be performed |in two hours good driving. The mansion at Léoube, dates from the time of Louis XIV., while Bréganson *Breganson.* though occupying the old Roman site of Pergantium is more modern in its general aspect. Nearly all the historical events, concerning the town of Hyères, are more or less connected with this ancient fort. As a strategical position, it commands all the anchorage of Hyères, and important modern fortifications are built on this headland.

The view here obtained is magnificent; all the islands of Hyères are seen in *enfilade*, and this explains their original name, the *Stœchades*;—the islands that follow one another, describing a sort of Indian file. Unfortunately, it is impossible within the province of this work to give even a brief description of the many historical, interesting, and beautiful places than can be visited from Hyères, particularly if the excursionist will venture to sleep one night on the road. From Bréganson there is no reason why the adventurous should not visit St. Tropez; and then Fréjus will naturally suggest itself, united with the names of Bormes and La Chartreuse. Then on the other side, and beyond Toulon, the celebrated Gorges d'Ollioules, Toulon itself and the ascent of the Coudon,—all will tempt the visitor. It is scarcely necessary to insist on the attractions of Toulon, but the walk back to Hyères along the coast which can be accomplished in an afternoon by good pedestrians is especially agreeable Few persons will care to return homewards without first visiting the Toulon Arsenal, the garden of St. Mandrier, the fort, the quays, and the quaint old town.

List of Excursions. The distances to the various excursions are given in M. Amédée Aufauvre's book on Hyères, and putting aside minute fractions, may be thus translated into English mileage.

Towards the south-west the distance to the Grotte des Fées is little more than a mile.

The summit of la Maunière, two and a half miles.
Costebelle, two and a half miles.
Pomponiana, four miles.
Carqueyranne, via Almanarre, six and a quarter miles.
The Colle Noire, nine miles.
Toulon, eleven miles.

To the south, the Plage du Ceinturon, is three and a half to four miles.

To the south-east the old Salins by the St. Tropez road is six and a quarter miles, the return by the Gapeau and the Pére Eternal road four and a half miles.

Bormettes is seven and a half miles.

Léoube, eleven and a half miles.

Bréganson, sixteen and a half miles.

Bormes, twelve and a half miles.

Chartreuse de la Verne, twenty-five miles.

Towards the north east, Décurgis two and a quarter miles.

The Oratoire, three and three quarter miles.

La Bravette, four and a quarter miles.

The Plan du Pont, five miles.

The distance to the Plan du Pont is reduced by half, if instead of passing by Décurgis, L'Oratoire and La Bravette, the mountain path is taken over the hill of La Sauvette which rises immediately behind the cemetery.

Pierrefeu is eleven and a half miles.

Towards the North West the distance to the Fenouillet by the Beauvallon road is four miles; but it must be borne in mind that the mountain itself is 980 feet high.

La Crau by Bayore and along the Béal four and a half miles.

Soullies Pont is seven and a half miles.

Chatreuse de Montrieux, seventeen miles and a half.

"THE GOLDEN ISLAND."

CHAPTER IX.

As advanced sentinels of the dark chain of mountains that stretches northward over the Mainland, the Island of Hyéres stand out boldly in the sea, sheltering the fruit-bearing coasts that are so near at hand. For centuries they have been the stepping-stones to the great country which is now called France. The merchant and the invader, the Phœnician and Saracen, both first landed on these islands, feeling their way towards the mainland. To the Romans they were known as the *Stœchades insulœ*, and Pliny wrote that from time immemorial coral fisheries existed round these islands, and the Gauls used this coral to ornament their shields. There are now three large islands. The first to the extreme east is known on account of its position as l'Ile du Levant, sometimes called l'Ile du Titan; then the Ile de Portcros, so named after its hollow port, *port-creux*, and finally Portquerolles, from the Gallo-Roman word, *olla*, pottery, the port for pottery—*Port Olles* To this list without mentioning the smaller islands or rocks such as Bagand and Rouband, I would add the Presqu'ile de Giens which has so evidently been joined to the mainland within recent years. This view, if accepted, has the rare advantage of enabling us to visit what to all intent and purposes is an island, without having to cross any water!

These island are all of the same geological formation as the Maures mountains. With respect, however, to its connection with the mainland, the peninsular of Giens is precisely an-alagous to the cap Cepet, that protects the approaches to Toulon. Both these ancient islands have only been recently joined to the mainland by narrow strips of sand thrown up by the sea and strengthened by the arts of man. Let us, therefore, proceed to visit, and this in a carriage, what was once the most westerly of the Strœchades islands. The distance is seven *The drive to* miles if we drive there by the Almanarre road *Giens.* and return by the Pesquiers. Nor will the nature of the road dispel the illusion that we are about to visit an island. To the right the waves dash up to the carriage wheels, and if the water a few feet to the left is more calm, it is nevertheless blue as the sea, salt as the sea, and rich with sea shells. But as the sand becomes dry and heavy, the coachman, to ease his horses, drives right into the water, where the ground is firmer, and the sea spray refreshes the horses' feet. At last, after a long, and to the horses a tedious journey, the mainland of the peninsular is reached, and a rough, steep twisting road, brings us to the little cluster of houses that constitute the village of Giens. From this elevation a grand picture of the broad southern sea unrolls itself. The ground slants abruptly down to the shore where some rugged rocks and a few palm trees form a wild outline against the blue waters and seething foam. In its main and most characteristic features this scene recalls the coasts of Africa and it is difficult to believe that we are still in Europe. The rocks of clay slate mingled with mica-schist glisten in the sun; splitting into thin layers, the mica stone might be mistaken for plaques of burnished tin or copper, gold or silver, according to the radation of the sun's light that plays upon it. Perhaps it was the red glow of the sun setting over these islands that first suggested the name of the Iles d'Or?

To the north of Giens, on the road to Sémaphore and near what is known as the port de la Madrague, a solitary rock standing in a field and reaching an altitude of twenty to twenty-five feet, may be observed. It is composed of a mixture of *A geological* quartz with a certain quantity of iron, which in *curiosity.* dissolving has discoloured the surface; then,

there are thin and irregular veins of yellow and brilliant
mica which seem to indicate that the quartz was formed
in a mica rock, and that its hardness enabled it to survive
the gradual decay of the surrounding land. Hence this
huge stone is probably the relic of a former geological
existence. The whole of the surrounding land is of a comparatively recent creation, this one rock stands witness to
the fact that the island was formerly made of a very different
material which was worn away by time and replaced by newer
land and stones. It is unfortunate, however, that there is no
one at Giens capable of understanding these very interesting
problems and of pointing them out to visitors. The walk to
the Sémaphore or telegraphic station situated at an altitude of
374 feet is agreeable and varied, while in the opposite or
easterly direction, a carriage can drive to the Tour-Fondue. It
is from this point that a boat crosses over to Porquerolles every
Monday, Thursday, Saturday, and Sunday, at 9.30 in the morning. Two good cannons and one solitary guardian defend the
little fortress in times of peace. From this point it is not
necessary to return to the village of Giens where beyond the
general view and the insignificant ruins of an old castle there
is nothing to be seen. A road slanting across the width of the
peninsular brings us to the easterly strip of land which connects
Giens with the shore, this is known as the Chemin des
Pesquiers, the name given to the salt marshes enclosed between
these two ribbons of sand. Here are the new Salins, which are
as important, though more modern, than the *vieux*   *Giens an*
Salins already described.   Both these strips of   *island.*
sand which wall off this marsh of salt water from the sea
were swept away during a storm in 1809, and Giens once
more became an island. The connecting link was only
re-established at great cost. The drive homewards is more
pleasant, the way wider, and lined with the sweet scented
tamarisk, the lenticus and rushes.   Opposite the Tour-
Fondue but on the northern side of the Peninsula, many

traces of Roman occupation will be found, both coarse and fine pottery, while the modern cemetery of the village occupies the site of an ancient burial ground. Further, the discovery of numerous flint instruments proves that during the age of stone Giens was inhabited.

To visit Porquerolles is at present a matter of some difficulty, but with a little management and by making plans in good time the expedition can be pleasantly organised. A letter or a telegram should be sent to M. Raymond, the proprietor of the Hotel du Progres, or to M. Roux, Maison Roux, ordering breakfast or dinner and retaining rooms, if it is intended to pass a night on the island. The principal object, however, is to order a boat to be sent at an early hour either to the Plage or the Salins, both of which points can be reached by train or by carriage. The journey from La Plage to Porquerolles is the shortest, but if the wind is fresh and blowing from an easterly direction, it is difficult and sometimes impossible to get on board from the little jetty that serves as a landing stage. At the *Sailing to* Salins on the contrary, there is a small harbour, *Porquerolles* and no difficulty will be experienced whatever the nature of the weather. If the wind is favourable, and blows hard, the journey from the Salins to Porquerolles can be accomplished in an hour and twenty minutes, but with an unfavourable wind or in a dead calm, the journey may last more than two hours. The scenery is, however, so magnificent, the air so fresh that the time will pass quickly. The little boat, with its crew of two or three men, also affords considerable distraction. To navigate these seas the skipper must possess extensive knowledge. He is familiar with every dent, every opening in the mountains, he is ever on the look out for those sudden gusts of wind, that render the navigation of the Mediterranean coasts a matter of considerable risk when entrusted to inexperienced hands. A slight sign, the bend of the trees on the mountain tops, the movements of some small distant cloud, give timely warning and the little boat is held ready for the sudden rush of wind. There is no record existing of any accident happening in the journey to Porquerolles, except on one occasion when a captain who had navigated in a large ship on the open sea, imagined that he could manage one of the little fishermen's boats plying between the islands. The result was that his general experience as a sailor could not save him from his want of local knowledge; and the captain who had braved the storms of the ocean was capsized in the narrow channel that separates Porquerolles and the mainland.

As we near the island, the water becomes more and more clear, and soon we notice, to either side of the little harbour, a semi-circular beach of unparalleled whiteness. One of these has been happily termed the *plage d'argent*; and *The Silver* the prospect of resting on the Silver Beach of the *Beach.* Golden Island, to enjoy the contemplation of the coral studded rocks that rise from the blue waters is irresistible. Nor are these beaches the only points offering themselves for the enjoyment of nature and repose. The island is divided into seven ranges of small hills, and in the numerous valleys thus created are walks sheltered from every wind, where the umbrella pines throw their deep shade over the path and mingle their balsamic odour with the scent of the thyme, myrtle and the tamarisk.

The island, also, is far more civilized than Giens. It has a military station where the convalescent soldiers from Algeria are placed unde the care of Dr. Bernard.

There are some fortifications, and it is probable that at an early date far more important defensive works will be constructed on this island, while the steamer plying to and fro from Toulon, bringing the provisions for the soldiers, shells for the artillery, etc., gives a certain life to the place. Finally, though not least, there is an admirable local museum, *The Museum.* entirely the creation of the military chaplain,

M. Ollivier. This gentleman is himself a good illustration
of the salubrious climate of the island. He had been
suffering from chronic laryngitis, and but little hope was
entertained of saving his life when he was sent to
Porquerolles. In three months' time, however, the scent of
the pines and the effects of the climate began to produce a
change; and this without the assistance of any medicine.
M. Ollivier has now resided for many years at Porquerolles,
enjoying good health; devoting his spare time, energy, and
profound scientific knowledge to collecting specimens of every
object of interest that can be seen on the island. Thus we have
in M. Ollivier's museum specimens of all the typical plants to
be gathered at Porquerolles, including such varieties as the
Delphinium requienii, the *Genista Linifolia,* the *Pelargonium
capitatum,* and such local specialities as the *Cistus olbiensis,* the
Cistus Porquerollensis and the *Galium minutulum,* which can
only be found on this spot. By the side of these plants, are
exposed the geological specimens that demonstrate the formation
of the rocks and the soil of the island; then there are a number
of shells collected on its shores, the fish caught within sight of
the island and finally the birds that settle under its foliage.
All these curiosities carefully stuffed, preserved and sorted in
scientific order and labelled with the Latin, the Vulgar French,
and the Provençal names, by which they are known, constitute
a most interesting demonstration of the resources of this small
but choice island. Among the birds, I noticed the *Merops
Apiaster,* or Guepier, the Bec Fin (*Troclodyte*), and the Stormy
Treasuses of the Island. Petrel. Here also are some magnificent specimens of
Porquerolles coral which Pliny described as being
the best commercial coral that could be obtained. Then there is
a pearl found in a Porquerolles shell, some good spunges from
the beach, and excellent specimens of the strange shell which is so
often compared to a donkey's foot. Nor has M. Ollivier limited
his researches to natural history. He has also a rich collection
of coins found in the island, and which might serve as a basis

for its history. There is not, however, a single Greek coin in this collection, but the Roman money, beginning with Augustus, includes ten out of the twelve Cæsars and all the principal Emperors down to Julian the Apostate. Then for about 300 years, during the Merovingian and Carlovingian periods, the island seems to have been deserted; no coins are found to testify to the presence of any inhabitants, but, soon after, there comes a number of Moorish coins, and then there are coins down to the present day of almost every reign, showing that the island was constantly peopled.

The probabilities are that Porquerolles, lying on the high road between eastern and western civilization, was inhabited in turn by a great variety of peoples, including the Ligurians, the Romans, and though there is no coin to testify to their presence—even the Greeks. It has already been mentioned in the chapter on the "History of Hyres," that Francis I. drove the *Past History.* Moors away from the island; it was then that the fortress was built that still dominates the village and can easily be seen even from Hyères. This structure would be of but little use now, for even at the beginning of the century during the Napoleonic wars, the English fleet sent several cannon balls crashing through its walls. The island now belongs to M. le Duc de Vicence, the son of the Marquis de Caulaincourt, the celebrated diplomatist of the First Empire.

Porquerolles is situated at a distance of nine miles from Hyères, so that the crossing, as the crow flies, would be only six miles, while the sea journey to Toulon is nearly eighteen miles. The island itself is more than six miles long, and nearly two miles broad. Yet in this small area a number of excursions may be made and a considerable diversity of scenery enjoyed. The southern side is especially picturesque, for here there is nothing to check the full force of the sea, and the waves come rolling in to break against precipitous rocks, and re-echo in the caverns they have worn in the stone. On the highest of these hills, at an elevation of 368 feet, a lighthouse commands the whole coast and the neighbouring islands. But it is generally admitted *Portcros* that the harbour of Portcros is even more picturesque. On this latter island the highest hill, reaching an altitude of 646 feet, will be found; and its port is admirably scooped out between rocks which form a natural protection against the wind.

It is, however, a wild country to visit, for Portcros cannot boast of fifty inhabitants; but, on the other hand, the inland is thickly populated with red and other partridges, snipe, pheasants, rabbits, hares, and in fact a multitude of game. It is the chosen land of the sportsman and the naturalist rather than of the cultivator. The distance from Portcros to the Plage, at Hyères, is twelve and a half miles, but it is easily reached from Porquerolles. In size, the island measures only two and a half miles in length and one and a half in width. Close by, the rock or island of Bagaud, which shelters the harbour of Portcros from the westerly winds, is little better than a rabbit warren. On the eastern side a very narrow channel, called la Passe des Grottes, on account of the rocky nature of the cliffs on either side, separates Portcros from l'Ile du Levant. It is the last of the series. In size it measures five miles by three and a half miles. This island is renowned as having offered a place of refuge to the Monge or Monk of *The man* the Iles d'Or, just as Porquerolles boasts of the pre- *with the* *Iron Mask.* sence of the Man with the Iron Mask; who, over come by sea-sickness was allowed to land for a short while on the island. The tower where he was imprisoned, the bench on which he slept, and the hook in the wall to which he was attached are still shown to visitors. They recall in an un-pleasantly vivid manner, the suffering endured in those days of arbitrary government, when men were made to spend their whole lives in prison without any sort of trial or explanation being given as to the offence committed.

There is not the same mystery surrounding the Monge who

lived on the Ile du Levant. He, at least, was not believed to be the rightful heir to the throne of France, compelled to wear an iron mask so as to conceal his likeness to Louis XIV. The Monge was simply a monk belonging to a noble Genoese *The Monge* family, who, in spite of his oath, became desperately *du Levant.* enamoured of a lady, and tried to console himself by the silent contemplation of nature, by writing verses, some of a very amorous description, by compiling a history, and by painting. He is described, by ancient chroniclers, as being " singular and perfect in all the sciences and languages. He wrote divinely every sort of letter, in the arts of illuminating he was an exquisite and a sovereign master." Many attempts were made to tempt this gifted author to leave his island retreat, but they all failed, and he died in the little monastery he had created in 1408.

The Ile du Levant though larger is less picturesque than its neighbours, and has not even as many inhabitants as Portcros. The Montagne des Pierres Blanches, is, however, 423 feet high, and the rocks and stones would be particularly interesting to the geologist and minerologist. Mica, talk, titanic iron, ameanthus, actinolite, every variety of tourmaline, etc., abound on all sides. The flora is also equally remarkable, and therefore, this island, in spite of its meagre resources and small population should be visited.

At Porquerolles life is easy and cheap,—eight francs a day at the Hotel du Progres ; and, if required as low as five francs at the Maison Roux ! For this very small sum, cleanliness, sufficient food and the pure wine of the island can be secured, together *Cheap* with the exquisite fish, fresh from the sea. Many *Living.* persons who cannot afford to live at Hyères might with advantage spend a few months at Porquerolles, from whence they could visit all the neighbouring islands returning in the evening of the same day. These pleasant excursions will suggest that after all Hercules did not endure any great hardship when he came here to pick the oranges,—that is, the golden apples,— from whence, it is said, the islands derive their present name.

CHAPTER X.

Modern Hyères consists, in the first place, of the long thoroughfare known indiscriminately either as the Boulevart, or the
Route Nationale, and running from the extreme east to the
extreme west of the town.   As is usually the case, the newer
and more fashionable portions of the town are at the west end;
yet the current has lost, at times, some of its force : there is the

*The Quar-
tier de
l'Orient.*   ebb as well as the flow. Thus, some sixteen
years ago, Mr Hope Scott, a relation of our
great novelist, determined to make Hyères
his home.   He bought an extensive estate to the east of
the Place de Strasbourg, and there on sites that are admirably
selected a number of elegant villas were built, and this district,
the Quartier de l'Orient, was becoming the fashionable quarter
of the town.   Unfortunately for the prosperity of Hyères, Mr
Hope Scott died, and his property could not be sold during the
minority of his children.   Once more the tide of progress began
to flow westward.

Below the Quartier de l'Orient, commencing at the Place de
la Rade and the Jardin Denis, and terminating at the end of the
street, is that part of the Route Nationale known as the Quartier
du Bon Puits.   This district has in no way changed of late years,
its picturesque and characteristic features are thoroughly

*The Bon
Puits.*   French. It bears the work a day appearance
of the busy part of a provincial town. Here
we lose all trace of the winter resort and
holiday aspect of the Riviera.   It is the Marais or the

Faubourg St. Antoine, and not the Champ Elysées of Hyères. Toiling under the shade of giant Oriental Plane trees, the cooper, the carpenter, the ironmonger, and smith, work in the open air. Rough country carts station on the road side, agricultural implements, a variety of contrivances for the irrigation of fields and the drawing of water, are exposed by the house doors, the whole bears the smiling, invigorating aspect of a district that works, of a population that earns what it enjoys; and, as such, is a relief to the mind and the eye accustomed to the listless appearance of the wealthy, idle, invalids who lounge about the foreign quarter.

Beyond this district, and still farther east; as we approach the open fields, we pass the handsome Villa de Luynes and the Chateaubriand dominates the road from an elevation. Several coquettish villas are now in construction on this point, designed with much original taste by M. Boyer. To the north of the main road, under the shelter of a range of small hills, commanding a magnificent view and extending for more than a mile, are a number of sites which will ultimately be covered with villas, and will constitute an important suburb of the town. In the meanwhile we have the Hotel du Beau Site which will prove a powerful reactive against the current running westwards. This hotel promises to become at once one of the most expensive and the most *The Beau Site.* luxurious of the Riviera. At the station, a bath ambulance chair will be in waiting for invalids. In this, the patient can lie down and, suspended by delicate springs, protected from every gust and every wind, be drawn gently, without shock or exposure to the hotel. Here a patent system, based on the documents left by the well-known Dr Tronchin, is applied to every room, by which the patient can take inhalations of tar, benzoin, tolu, turpentine, etc., etc., according to his doctor's order. The temperature, by means of ventilation between the ceilings, will be maintained at 58 Fahr., in all the passages of the hotel. Balls, concerts, a military band

in the garden during meals, and a variety of other gratuitous
entertainments are to follow in rapid succession during the
whole season, and are to be enjoyed not only by the inhabitants
of the hotel but by numerous and distinguished guests recruited in all the villas and hotels of the town.

Returning westwards, a small road, running parallel with the
Bon Buits, called the Rue du Midi, has several villas which are
generally inhabited by French families; indeed, the whole of
the east end is more essentially the French quarter of Hyères
Nevertheless, at the Hotel des Etrangers, which is close by, there
are a number of English families who have learnt to appreciate
the good cuisine and management of this well-known establishment. Opposite the end of the Rue du Midi, commences the
Avenue des Palmiers which runs from this point to the Avenue
de l'Almanarre or the Boulevart de la Gare, as it will be called.
This magnificent thoroughfare is planted with sixty monumental palms which were brought over from
The avenue of Palms. Malaga not many years ago. Though still
young it is easy to see that they are much
finer specimens than those of the Place des Palmiers,
but the latter in consequence of their age and altitude, look
more picturesque. The most interesting building in this
Avenue is undoubtedly the Chateau Farnous now the Hotel du
Parc. Its rooms still retain some of their former palatial
grandeur, and are certainly exceptionally elegant and comfortable; while the surrounding garden has, if anything, improved.
When, at the beginning of this century, any visitors of special
distinction came to Hyères, they generally occupied this
Chateau, and among other celebrated personages Queen
Christina of Sweden, the sister of Napoleon I., resided here
for some time and became a victim to the skill and daring of
the renowned thief Moutone.

This local Fra Diavolo, was a man of the most refined
manners and handsome appearance. Introducing himself as a
foreign nobleman, he gained access to the most fashionable

society of Hyères and Toulon, and did not fail to become an intimate acquaintance of the royal household established at the Château Farnous.   Paying his addresses simultaneously to the Queen and her principal maid-servant, this audacious bandit contrived to gain admittance *A Local Fra Diavolo.* one night to the royal bed-chamber, where he soon collected all the crown diamonds and made good his escape.   He was only captured two years later, while dancing among the élite of the local society, at one of the Admiralty balls at Toulon,

In the Avenue des Palmiers there are several elegant villas, the old casino, now let out in apartments, and the new English church, which like most similar structures is insufficiently ventilated.   The church, therefore, becomes very close during service, and is a cause of *The English Church.* considerable danger and injury to the con- sumptive patients, who will persist in thus crowding together.   The bad ventilation of the church and the hotel dining rooms during table d'hôte are indeed responsible for much of the mischief done, the accidental colds contracted, which go so far to destroy the good effects of the climate.

From the Boulevart de la Gare to the Place des Palmiers the Route Nationale passes by the Hotel des Ambassadeurs, a hand- some building constructed only ten years ago and admirably sheltered by the old town and castle hill which it faces.   Close to and equally well-placed is the Hotel de l'Europe an essentially French hotel, with French and Provençal cooking and more moderate charges.   Now we arrive at the Place des Palmiers, which for long has been the glory of Hyères, but is destined to be completely eclipsed by the new enterprises of the Municipality and private speculators.   The palms were planted in 1835, and have therefore *The Eng-lish Quarter* reached a great altitude, and there is a pretty garden open at the foot of the place.   It is here that the band plays every week; the sun falls directly on the Place

and its seats are warmed by its genial light. A fine panorama
stretches out in front, embracing the mountains to the south,
the sea and the island of Porquerolles. A little further on is
the Hotel des Iles d'Or and the West End with its numerous
villas. At this point the Route Nationale turns towards the
north-west and affords a magnificent view of the setting sun
through the palm leaves that wave in the foreground from the
terrace des Palmiers in front of the hotel. Here are a number
of modern villas where apartments of all sizes are to be obtained
and which the English usually frequent. The district is
generally called the quartier des Iles d'Or.

From the Hyères of the present to the Hyères of the future,
the period of transition will be of but short duration, and the
great changes to be realized will place the town on, at least, a
footing of equality with the most popular resorts of the Riviera.
Indeed, the plan of the improvements is more extensive and
grand in its general outline than anything which has been
attempted elsewhere. Putting aside, for the moment, the
projects of the Municipality, for which a loan of £60,000 has
been contracted, the town is indebted to private initiative for
the conception of six new boulevards of which four are actually
in the course of construction, and will be officially inaugurated
in the autumn of this year. This gigantic undertaking will be
the regeneration of the entire English quar-
*The New
Boulevarts* ter. Nearly opposite the Hotel des Iles d'Or,
at the point of the angle formed by the
Rue Jean Natte and the Boulevart, or Route Nationale, commences the first of these boulevarts. A viaduct 656 feet in
length, now almost completed, will allow the new road to slope
gently down towards the plain, cutting across the country, and
reaching in a perfectly straight line, the railway station, from
which point it will be ultimately prolonged to La Plage, at the
seaside. This will not only shorten the distance from the
English quarter to the station, but will present a striking
spectacle to the astounded gaze of the traveller as he alights

from the train. For the distance of about a mile, he will be able to gaze up a magnificent avenue, sixty-five feet broad and shaded on either side by monumental palm trees. There will be planted in this and the corresponding thoroughfare no less than three hundred palms; and when these have had time to take firm root in the soil, and to develop their majestic branches, the effect produced will be unparalelled. Crossing this, the Avenue d'Albion, as it will be called, and at about two thirds distance from the town, a second and shorter boulevart running in a transversal direction will join the Rue St. Anne with the quartier Jean Natte and the Roubeau. This thoroughfare will be fortyfeet wide and as it cuts through what is now known as the Jardin Beauregard, it will be named after the late M. de Beauregard, formerly mayor of Hyères and Councillor General for the department of the Var. At the point where the Avenue de Beauregard and the Avenue d'Albion meet, a *rond point* will be made with a handsome monumental fountain some thirty feet in height, so that the play of the waters may be seen from the entire length of both the avenues. To be in keeping with the grandeur of this scheme a treaty has been concluded with the Municipality by which the width of the Rue de St. Anne is to be increased to forty feet. As the Rue St. Anne runs down by the Place des Palmiers this will necessitate the moving of the huge palm tree on the eastern extremity of this place; an operation of no small cost and difficulty.

While these works are in progress to the south of the Boulevart National a bold effort is made to the north of this the main thoroughfare. On a higher level, there is the Avenue des Eucalyptus, a somewhat deserted spot as it cannot be easily reached; but now this avenue is to be continued through the gardens at the back of the Hotel des Iles d'Or and a portion of the mountain has been *New Villas* cut away so as to create a carriage road branching off near the Post Office and passing between the original and elegant villas Marie Louise and Tour Jeanne

which are among M. Chapoulart's chef d'Œuvres, up towards
the avenue in question. Nor is this all, there are further
plans also due to private initiative which will render the
sheltered base of the Chateau Hill accessible to the builder
of villas, and to the carriages of excursionists.

What, however, is perhaps even more remarkable in these
efforts due to private enterprise are the very excellent rules
which are to govern the property thus created, to the very great
advantage of all concerned. In all these new thoroughfares, a
properly constructed sewer will be laid down. No house or
land will be let, or sold, or building lease granted, unless gas is
laid on and the company's drinking water taken in. No supply
of well-water can be free from the risk of contamination, and, therefore, for the preservation of
Admirable Regulations the public health, the drinking of the company's
water is rendered compulsory on all who
desire to live on this estate. It is further required that where
shops are to be opened the gas shall be kept burning till nine
in the evening, a rule which will greatly contribute towards the
gaiety of the district   Again, and so as not to spoil the general
appearance of the quarter, no division walls between gardens or
villas will be allowed.   Greenery is so easily grown that there
is no excuse for the building of a garden wall in such a country.
Finally, it must be added that in the building of houses on this
estate, no connection will be allowed with the sewers unless the
pipe used for this purpose is properly trapped with a siphon or
some other equally effective contrivance.

The frontage available for building purposes giving on to
these new boulevarts will amount to 13,120 feet extending over
an area of about eighteen hectares, or about forty-five acres, with
carefully drained and watered avenues, where numerous
seats will be placed under the shade of the palm trees
and near fountains that cool the atmosphere
Fields for Speculation, In the Avenues d'Albion and de Beauregard
there will be thirty-six benches and an ample

supply of gas lamps. Many of the building sites thus created command splendid views, and the development of this great estate will give rise to life and movement, speculation and building, to the opening of new shops, trades and industries, which will all tend to regenerate and transform the entire town.

The Municipality on their side propose spending the £60,000 they have been allowed to raise in the creation of a handsome boulevart leading from the centre of the town to the railway station. The Place des Palmiers and *Municipal* the Place Massillon are to be enlarged and a *Improve-* model market built on the latter square. A *ments,* new street is to be pierced through the old town, various roads improved, canals reconstructed, a new cemetery prepared, and a new school built. Finally, the villa, and Jardin Denis, have been purchased by the Municipality. The villa will be pulled down so that the garden may be seen from the place de la Rade and at the other end a Casino is to be built.

A company is now in course of formation for the creation of this Casino, and the programme presented to the public appears wonderfully complete. M. Chatron, the celebrated architect of Lyons, who built the Theatre de Bellecour in that city, has already completed his design for the Hyères Casino, and it promises to become an elegant and fanciful structure. Reading rooms, lecture and concert rooms, permanent exhibition of fine arts in the saloons, horticultural competitions in the gardens balls, parties, children's parties and games, theatre, a band of thirty-five performers, fire *The Future* works, illuminations, a restaurant, managed *Casino,* by a celebrated Paris chef, a table d'hote and dining rooms for four hundred persons are on the programme. We are also promised gaming tables so far as the law will authorise them, to which none but the members of first class European clubs will be admitted. In connection with the casino it is also proposed to organize international shooting matches at long

ranges, and pigeon shooting, horse races, fox hunting regattas
in the Rade d'Hyères, shooting and battues in the marshes
and forests belonging to the Municipality. Altogether we have
here a programme which, if only half realized, will make Hyères
as gay a town as any on the Riviera.

More modest, but none the less useful, is the association just
The Eng-
lish Club,
formed by some of the leading English
residents for the purpose of creating an English
reading-room and circulating library on the
basis of a club. Apartments at the elegant Villa Marie
Louise have already been secured. These are near to the
tennis ground which will now be managed in connection with
this newer association. Ladies, as well as gentlemen, will be
allowed to participate in the benefits of the library and reading
room, and doubtless this institution will soon become a regular
English club managed by Englishmen according to English
principles and customs.

While these improvements are progressing within the town
itself considerable activity has been displayed in the neighbouring districts of Carqueryanne and Costebelle, particularly now that the water of the company can be brought to any
The Ermit-
age Estate,
part of the country. A group of Englishmen are
negociating for the purpose of a large tract of land
at Costebelle near to the Ermitage Hotel, and now
called the Ermitage Estate. It extends over the southern slope
of a hill at an altitude varying from a hundred to three hundred
feet overlooking the Mediterranean, which is at a distance of
only a mile. As arrangements have been made with an
architect of high repute to draw up plans for villas to be built
for a certain fixed sum without any trouble to the owner, it is
probable that this spot will soon become peopled by a colony of
English. Already a road is in course of construction through
the estate, and the land is divided into building plots of different

sizes, so that here again we have evidently the beginning of a new developement in the greatness and prosperity which is in store for Hyères and its neighbourhood.

Half way between Costebelle and Carqueryanne the magnificent Chateau or Palace of San Salvador will now be soon completed and will give new life to the whole sea coast. It would be difficult to find a more lovely aspect than that presented by these shores, and there are admirable sites for villa building for those who do not fear the neighbourhood of the Mediterranean and who wish to live amid pine clad hills. At the same time there are some ugly walls that run down the side of these hills which spoil the view and would at once be pulled down by any public spirited proprietor. The rights of property are associated with certain moral duties and responsibilities, and the privileges of the individual should not be allowed to mar the sublime scenery which nature has created for the benefit of all.

Villas on the Shore.

Again there is the project of creating an asylum or hospital for strumous children on the exposed site selected by Dr Vidal between the Salins des Pesquiers and the extreme end of the Plage du Ceinturon. On this isolated and weather-beaten spot, these unfortunate children while recovering their spirits, health, and vitality, under the stimulating influence of the sea breezes, would not in anyway interfere with the gaiety and prosperity of Hyères. On the contrary, the success attending the treatment of the poor would bring the children of the rich to the same locality thus augmenting the number of foreigners whose presence enriches the country. The administrations of the Bureaux de Bienfaisances of Paris, are beginning to take the matter up, and it is probable that the scheme will be ultimately carried out to the great satisfaction of all who feel that

A word for the Poor,

the rich should not benefit alone by the exceptional climatic advantages Hyères offers in the cure of disease. It will be, indeed, a sign of real prosperity and real greatness when, side by side with the luxurious residences where the middle and upper classes prolong their existence and modify the suffering entailed by their diseases, asylums will be built for the benefit of the poorer and industrial classes, whose labour is the foundation of all wealth.

THE END

APPENDIX.

ADDRESSES AND GENERAL INFORMATION.

TOWN HALL.

For matters relating to the municipal government of the town : watering of the roads, drainage, scavenging, certificates of birth, death, or marriages, civil marriages, inspection of meats, and food generally, reclamations relating to the wholesomeness of the same, etc, etc, apply to the Town Hall (Mairie), Place Massillon.

The Mayor may be seen personally every day between 10 and 11 a.m.

LAW COURT.

The Palais de Justice de Paix is on the Place de la République. The sittings of the Tribunal are held on the Tuesdays and Fridays, the Court opening at 10 a.m. On all the other days the Judge of the Peace may be seen at his office,—adjoining the Court, from ten o'clock till neon. M. Gilbert Roux, junior, is the clerk of the Court.

POLICE STATION

Is situated on the ground floor of the Mairie, or Town Hall, and open every day, Sundays included, from seven in the morning till midnight. All information and complaints relating to offences against the common law, acts of violence, thefts, etc, should at once be communicated to this office.

POST OFFICE.

The Post Office is a few steps beyond the Place des Palmiers. It is a small one-storied house which will probably be re-built at an early date. The office is opened from 8 a.m. to 7 p.m. on week days. On Sundays and feast days it is closed from noon to 3 o'clock, and finally closed at 5 p.m. LETTERS FOR ENGLAND should be posted before 5 p.m. (town time), and will be delivered in London by the first post in the morning of the day after the morrow. But as all letters posted Friday afternoon reach London Sunday morning they will be delivered as soon if posted on Saturday, while, with respect to the receipt of letters, Tuesday corresponds with the London Sunday. For the day Calais mail, letters should be posted at Hyères before 6.5. a.m., when they will reach London on the evening of the following day. The other levies made are at 9.5. a.m. and 2.15. p.m. All four levies take letters for both directions, eastwards for Mentone and Italy, westwards for Marseilles. LETTERS FROM ENGLAND are distributed at 11.30. a.m., and since the institution of the *train eclair* the second mail travels more rapidly, so that the letters and papers are distributed at 2.45. p.m. Thus a letter posted in London on, for instance, Monday afternoon, in time for the evening mail, will be delivered at Hyères at about mid-day the following Wednesday, while a letter posted during Monday night in time for Tuesday morning's mail will reach only a few hours later, and be distributed at Hyères at about three o'clock Wednesday afternoon. Hence as London morning papers are published at 4 a.m., they can be forwarded by the morning mail, and the previous day's London paper can be obtained at Hyères after three in the afternoon. Of course if delay arises in crossing the channel, or on the railway line, these rules no longer hold good; but considering the great distance of the journey these accidents do not often occur. Snow on the French line, a storm or a dense fog in the channel, are the most to be feared.

TELEGRAPHIC OFFICE.

Despatches may be forwarded by wire any time from 8 a.m. to 9 p.m. to all parts of the world. The Telegraph Office is almost next door to the Post Office, and there is every probability that the hours for sending off despatches will be extended to midnight. The cost of a telegram to England is four francs for twenty words, and one halfpenny, five centimes, per word to any part of France.

PUBLIC WORSHIP.

Mass is celebrated on Sundays at the Church dedicated to St. Louis, Place de la République, at 6.30., 8, and 9.10. a.m. High Mass at 11.30. a.m., and Vespers at 3 p.m.—The Church of St. Paul, Place St. Paul, Mass at 6 and 7 o'clock. Mass is also celebrated at 7 o'clock at the Civil Hospital and at the Chapelle de l'Ermitage at 8 o'clock.

THE FRENCH PROTESTANT service is held at ten o'clock at the Temple des Palmiers.

THE CHURCH OF ENGLAND service is held on Sundays at Christ Church, Avenue des Palmiers, at 10.30. a.m. and 3 p.m.

Wednesdays and Fridays, Church Holydays and saints' day at 10.30. a.m.

Holy communion every Sunday and saints' day at 10.30. a.m.

The church library is open every Wednesday after service. Subscriptions, 5 fr.

Attendance is given at the same time for allotting seats. For other information see the English Chaplain, The Rev P. E. Singer, Villa des Orangers.

CLUBS.

The principal club is the Cercle d'Hyères, on the Place de la Rade, immediately above the Café du Siècle. The subscription fee for strangers is 20 francs per month, or 60 francs per season.

This club is neutral in politics, is the most luxurious institution at Hyères of its kind. In the daytime it will be found a quiet resort for reading the French papers; but in the evening there is card-playing, not to say a little gambling, as is indeed the case in all French clubs. On the whole, this is the club that will suit the average English visitor best.

The Cercle de Provence is essentially a political and clerical institution. Its object is to unite the local aristocracy and gentry who profess Legitimist, or, at least, Reactionary and strong clerical tendencies, with the working classes. Hence the entrance fee is 60 francs and 10 francs respectively. A certain number of workmen, by joining this institution have obtained employment and patronage from the wealthier members whose views they profess to adopt. Similar clubs, generally bearing the same name, and certainly organized for the same party purposes exist in most of the towns of Provence.

The Cercle de la Méditerranée, is a middle class or tradesman's club, the members being composed principally of the shopkeepers of Hyères. The fee is 20 francs or 5 francs per month. Formerly it was purely a social club and though now its members hold different views on politics, they nevertheless unite and bring considerable pressure to bear on matters concerning local administration and are important factors in the election of municipal councilors. Their influence is used on the whole in a Liberal sense.

The Cercle de l'Industrie, Place Strasbourg, Fee 5 francs; Subscription 12 francs per annum. A political, radical and working men's club. It possesses a good library of 500 volumes. Foreigners are admitted gratuitously and will be received with great courtesy. During the latter days of the Empire this club struggled painfully for existence, but now it forms a compact body of ardent politicians who are more powerful at an election than any other club in the town. The more advanced members of the Cercle de la Méditerranée also belong to this club, together with several doctors and other members of the Liberal professions desirous of participating in the active political work done by this society.

PUBLIC LIBRARIES.

At the Mairie there was a library of about 1200 volumes, but it is now in a state of disorder. As, however, M. Denis left his valuable library to the town and M. Laurent followed this example, there is now question of appointing a public librarian, who will unite all these resources and form an important collection. In the meanwhile, the library attached to the Church of St Louis is the most important of the town, and possesses about 4000 volumes. Then there is the library connected with the English church for English works, and the good though small French library of the Cercle de l'Industrie. Madame Trotobat, Place des Palmiers, lets books on hire and has a number of standard English works and novels.

DOCTORS.

ENGLISH PRACTITIONERS.

Dr G. GRIFFITH, 19, Boulevard National, next door to the Hotel des Iles d'Or. One of the most experienced English physicians on the Riviera; his local practice and experience of the climate, its peculiar effects in disease, and the special complaints of the South, extending over twenty-one years.

Dr W. P. BIDEN, Villa Platane, 22, Route Nationale. Practising in partnership with Dr Griffith.

FRENCH PRACTITIONERS.

Dr VIDAL may be mentioned first, on the ground that he has the largest French practice, and attends several English families, and also because he is the doctor of the hospital and of the custom house officials—both government appointments. Route Nationale, at the beginning of the Bon Puits, or easterly district.

Dr CHASSINAT, knight of the legion of honour, laureate of the Paris faculty, Villa Pierre-lisse, place Cafabre.

Dr CESSENS, from Aix-les-Bains, Maison Contant, 3 Place de la Republique.

Dr DECUGIS, 27 rue Massillon.

Dr Jaubert, Inspector of the waters of Gréoulx. Maison Maurel, Avanue de l'Almanarre.

Dr Kastas, Maison Maurel Avenue de l'Almanarre.

Dr Laube, knight of the Legion of honour, naval physician. Route Nationale, speaks English.

Dr Ed. Loniewski, Route Nationale.

Dr Marquez from Colmar (Alsace), 8 rue des Porches.

Dr Charles Roux, 167, Route Nationale, Maison Mauriser.

Dr Verignon, villa Leon Antoinette Boulevart d'Orient.

At Porquerolles.—Dr A. Bernard, Medical Officer of the Dépot of Convalescents from Africa.

CHEMISTS.

M. Massel, Place Portalet, whose English assistant dispenses the drugs imported direct from Messrs Bell and Co., of Oxford-street, London.

M. Audibert, Pharmacie Centrale, Place Portalet.

M. Alexandre Castueil, Route Nationale, Mason Aréne.

M. Marius Castueil, Place de la Rade.

English Chemist, Villa Marie Lousie, Route Nationale.

MONTHLY NURSE.

Madame Othon, First-class diploma from the faculty of Montpellier. 10 rue Massillon.

NURSES.

The Sisters of the Esperance :—Maison Serre, place des Palmiers. Most of the hotel keepers are acquainted with lay nurses who can sit up at night with the sick. But there would be a good opening at Hyères for two or three English trained nurses.

HOSPITAL.

The Hotel Dieu : to the extreme west of the town, and the Boulevart National. There are here a few private rooms where board, lodging, and medical attendance can be obtained for five francs a day. The wards are of course opened free to the destitute, and are exceptionally well aired and capacious. The drains, however, are very imperfect, and in fact are a blot to another-wise admirable institution.

BANKS.

The English Bank of Hyères. English Cheques, Letters of Credit, etc., on the leading London and American Banks cashed.

Desposit accounts opened and very favourable terms allowed.

Crédit Hyèrois, and the Banque de Nice.

SOLICITORS.

M. Ancey, rue Nationale, Maison Brunet Dronet. M. Paget Georges, Place de la Republique. 3.—M. Louis Patteson, Place de la Rade.

BAILIFFS.

M. Digne, Place de la République. Maison Curel, M. Reboul, rue de la République.

PROFESSORS.

W. Henley Chater, M.A., St. Johns College, Oxford, late Scholar, Classical Honourman, and of Lincolns Inn, Barrister at Law. Preparation for the Universities and other Examination. Address at the English Bank.

Professor of Languages—M. Payan, 12, Rue St. Claire.

THE WATER COMPANY.

The Compagnie Générale des Eaux, better known as The Compagnie Parisienne, is an anonymous society possessing a capital of £800,000. The supply of drinking water for the town of Hyères and to private residences is undertaken by this company; and all requests, complaints, etc, relating to the water should be addressed to the offices of this administration, situated on the first floor of the Maison Bessen, Avenue d'Almanarre. The Plumber of the company is on the ground floor of same house.

THEATRE.

Place Strasbourg; performances once or twice a week, generally by the company from the Toulon theatre,

BATHS.

Rue St. Anne, Place des Palmiers for 1 franc, and baths can be brought to the house or hotel for 3 francs; also in the Rue de Midi; where sulphurous and other medical baths may be obtained.

DILIGENCES OR OMNIBUSES.

The diligence for Toulon starts from M. Salust' stables, near the Place de la Rade, at 6 a.m., and reaches La Pauline in time to catch the train that starts from Toulon at 7 a.m. for Nice. Another diligence leaves Hyères at 8 a.m. and correspond but not so accurately, with the 10 o'clock Nice train, still many travellers prefer waiting an hour at La Pauline to starting earlier and waiting longer at Toulon. There are other diligences at 11 a.m. and 3 p.m. from Hyères to Toulon. The journey should be performed in an hour and three quarters, if there are not many stoppages on the road. The fare is one franc, and 1 franc, 50 c. for the *coupé*. The diligences from Toulon to Hyères start at 8 and 11 a.m., and at 3.30. and 6 p.m.

There is an omnibus that goes daily to Carqueyranne leaving Hyères at 11 a.m. and 5 p.m., and returning from Carqueyranne at 8 a.m. and 3 p.m fares 50 centimes.

For Les Salins the omnibus start at 10.30 a.m. and 5 p.m. returning at 7 a.m. and 1.30 p.m. The traffic on this line is not so great, and therefore, though the distance is much shorter, the fare is one franc.

CARRIAGES.

These cannot be hired by the hour but must be taken for the day or for the afternoon; the cheapest being a carriage with a single horse for 7 francs and with two horses for 12 francs

To this a gratuity to the coachman must be added. A landau may be hired, with two horses and reserved exclusively for the use of the person by whom it is retained for 500 francs a month; a price which is considerably below the charge made at Nice or Cannes. There are three persons who let carriages :—M. Jules Armand, Boulevard de Strasbourg. M. Julien Eyffren, Route Nationale. M. Louis, Route Nationale. Omnibuses for picnics, holding 12 or more persons, may also be obtained.

MARKET.

Place Massillon. fish and vegetable market every morning. The fish, at least, is generally all disposed of before noon. The fresh sardines and small fish are as a rule sold at five pence a pound, while the larger fish is worth a franc a pound. The fish is always very fresh, sometimes still alive.

PROVISIONS.

These are ample and tolerably cheap. The groceries are much dearer than in England the meat a little cheaper, and vegetables very much cheaper. A good sound dinner wine, if bought in the *bom bonne* and made from the local grapes, can be obtained for five pence the litre, and the bom bonne contains generally either 8 or 22 litres. It would not pay to adulterate this wine, and the same cannot be said of more expensive sorts. Of course oil and vinegar are excellent and cheap. The poultry is imported from Toulouse and La Bresse, and is therefore very good. The neighbouring peasantry will not kill their poultry but keep them for their own consumption or for eggs. Many shops sell English biscuits, tinned Australian meats, and various well-known English specialties such as corn flour, pickles, etc., These are however dear, for heavy duties are imposed and large profits made. Altogether life is easy at Hyères for those who live in the French style, and an English family, of moderate means, with someone able to speak French and able to bargain, would find the cost of provisions, on the whole, cheaper here than in London. The meat supply is fairly good but it is too fresh when offered for sale and should be hung some time before it is eaten. Each joint bears the stamp of the slaughter house inspector, and this is a guarantee for the soundness of the meat. If the inspector has any doubt he calls in the neighbouring veterinary and, as all the cattle are killed at the large slaughter house situated at a little distance from the town, they are held under control and this system offers considerable sanitary advantages. Prime joints are sold at a franc or ten-pence a pound, and the French half kilo or pound weighs a little more than the English pound, whereas in the West-end of London the same joints would cost a shilling the English pound. Fillet of beef and rump steak cost more, namely 1s. 3d. the lb; and the favourite French meat veal is also dear. On the other hand, excellent loin, mutton chops, are only charged tenpence the pound, though in the West-end of London they would cost 1s. 3d. or 1s. 4d. Vegetables it is hardly necessary to point out are exceptionally excellent and cheap. During last season, in the month of April and May, special trains comprising in all 150 waggons conveyed every day from the Riviera to Paris the early vegetables and fruits which in the North are considered such great and expensive luxuries. The commune of Hyères was able to fill daily 37 out of the 150 waggons loaded with *primeures*. Thus it is that even in April bundles of asparagus comprising about sixty small but excellent beads may be obtained for sixpence. At the same time new potatoes and peas, and salads are excessively cheap, and in fact become stale before they are even tasted in England. Towards the end of April strawberries and cherries follow in their turn, and it is odd on returning to London, to find the fruit which was over ripe at Hyères barely introduced at home and sold at fabulous prices instead of being a drug in the market. All these circumstances contribute to render life cheap at Hyères; but it cannot be too much insisted upon that both for the sake of health and of economy the resident should seek to do at Rome as the Romans. Let his diet in Provence resemble, at least to some extent, the diet of the Provençal. The heavy English cooking, and above all the strong alcohols consumed at home, must be vigorously abjured. Light beverages, fish, fresh crisp, newly cut salads, with plenty of the oil for which the country is noted, French bread; and in fact as far as possible, the native dishes, the native style of cooking are more suitable. The inhabitants of a country invariably know best what is best suited to their climate. It is because the English too often fail to carry out this maxim that they find their digestive faculties impaired and the cost of living dearer than they had anticipated.

SHOPS.

It would be expedient to secure a complete outfit of clothes before leaving England, as the shops at Hyères are of a modest description so far as articles of general wear are concerned. From this rule we should except boots, which are always better anywhere out of England; and it is high time that English ladies should cease to offend the artistic taste of their foreign critics by the notorious inelegance of their ill fitting boots and shoes. There are in the Hyères shops a few specialties that will attract the visitors. The sunshades are cheap, serviceable, sometimes elegant and always indispensable. The walking sticks and canes made with the branches of the palm trees, twisted and polished, are peculiar; fancy articles made with olive wood are less rare. There is some pretty china, and the rough Provencal pottery is wonderfully cheap and artistic. The large green water jugs which the peasant women carry are most picturesque, and worth from fourpence to sixpence.

The jars for flowers, the table water jugs, and many other articles are remarkable; while the earthenware cooking utensils, stewpans and saucepans from a penny to sixpence each, according to size, are most useful, and it is easier to cook in them than in the more expensive metallic implements of the North. The dried wild flowers and grasses are often sold for the trimming of bonnets, etc.; and for Palm Sunday the confection-ers sell little bamboo sticks ornamented with gold paper, and hung with preserved fruits and sweetmeats, which the children carry to church and subsequently devour. There is also a brisk trade in light wooden boxes and cotton wool for packing and despatching flowers by post; these should not cost more than three half-pence or two-pence.

There is a general tendency here as elsewhere on the part of the shopkeepers to raise their prices when dealing with a fo-reigner. This should be resisted by every means both for the sake of the foreigners themselves and for the natives of Hyères who estrange visitors by this shortsighted policy. At the same time, it must be recognized that many English persons, by reason of their stiff, haughty, unbending behaviour towards the tradesmen invite extortion. A more civil, communicative and friendly bearing on the part of purchaser would soon bring about compensating leniency on the part of the shopman. In this democratic country, where caste has been abolished, the tradesman, the workman, the peasant, expect, and are gene-rally treated with the same deference and civility as the lord or plutocrat. This great and fundamental difference between England and France many English have failed to appreciate, and consequently their behaviour has rendered them unpopular with the natives, who only tolerate their presence in conse-quence of the money they are able to make out of them. Never-theless the Hyères shopman is, as a rule, very civil, but his com-plaints are loud and bitter against the English when he has an opportunity of expressing his feelings. English persons, for instance, often enter a shop, give their orders in a loud com-manding tone of voice, never trouble themselves about the other and perhaps more modest customers, who, being first to come, have the right to be first served. There is no apology offered for the interruption, no sign of acknowledgement, no good-day, exchanged with the tradesman. The Englishman or woman sails out of the shop as if ignoring the existence of other fellow

135

creatures standing by; who, on their side, shrug their shoulders at our bad manners, and console themselves with the extent of the order received and the exorbitant price charged. A few such persons in an English colony are enough to turn a whole town against us, and unfortunately this bad, purse-proud behaviour is not a rare occurrence among the English customers of the Hyères shops; and the innocent suffer too often from the impression produced by these numerous and obnoxious compatriots.

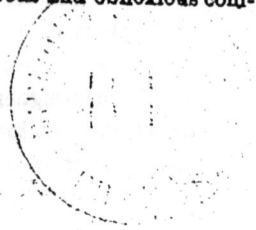

PRINTED AND PUBLISHED BY J. EVANS AND COMPANY, 11, BRIDGE STREET, (OPPOSITE HOUSES OF PARLIAMENT,) WESTMINSTER, LONDON, S.W.

INTERNATIONAL OFFICES,

M. V. DONGOIS,

AGENT

2 Avenue de la Gare Hyères.

English travellers will find at M. Dongois' " Bureaux Internationaux" the easiest and cheapest means and rates for the transport by fast and slow trains of small parcels, flowers, fruits, luggage and merchandise of any kind.

Information can only be obtained at the following "Bureaux Internationaux":—NICE, 34, Avenue de la Gare; MENTONE, 9, Rue Saint Charles; CANNES, 13, Rue de Grasse; HYERES, 2, Avenue de la Gare; MONACO, Rue Antoinette; SAN-REMO (Italy), Corso Emanuele.   875

ANTIQUITIES.

MAISON BENOIST,

29, Route Nationale, 29.

ANCIENT & MODERN CURIOSITIES
AND OBJECTS OF ARTS.

CHINESE, JAPANESE
PORCELAIN & OTHER ARTICLES.

Mirrors, Clocks, Old Furniture.

MARSEILLES POTTERY
BOTH NEW AND OLD.

ROMAN BRONZES AND OTHER ANTIQUITIES.

RELICS AND VARIOUS RARE AND
CHOICE WORKS OF ART.

MODERATE PRICES.

871 5.80

HOTEL ET PENSION DES HESPERIDES,

ONE OF THE MOST COMFORTABLE AND ECONOMICAL HOTELS IN THE SOUTH OF FRANCE.

Situated in the English—that is, in the healthiest—quarter of Hyères. Highly recommended; First class accommodation.

APARTMENTS WITH BOARD, FROM 7 FRANCS TO 10 FRANCS PER DAY

According to the Floor and Room taken.

ENGLISH NEWSPAPERS.

W. MARTIN, PROPRIETOR.

☞ *A fine Avenue of well-developed Palm Trees grow in the open air in front of this Hotel.—Reference to English Visitors may be had on application.*

757.4.80

CH. HUBER & Co.,

M. KNODERER (MANAGER),

HORTICULTURISTS AT HYÈRES (VAR), FRANCE.

GOLD MEDALS

FOR THE

PURITY AND EXCELLENCE OF THEIR SEEDS.

SEEDS of new growths, of rare plants, annuals, perennials, hot house and other plants, trees and shrubs and bulbs.

PLANTS—Musa Ensete, Cycas circinalis, Palms, Dracaena, Eryngium, Citrus, Pomegranates, Bamboos, Oleanders, etc.

DRIED GRASSES for nosegays, garlands, ornamental vases, trimming of bonnets, etc.

CUT FLOWERS—Roses, violets (Wilson & Czar), sold per kilogramme.

BOXES OF FLOWERS FOR LONDON sent by Parcels' express, maximum weight 10lbs, freight only 4. s., Rose-buds, violets, and other spring and summer flowers, cut but still fresh and in good condition, can thus be delivered in London during the months of November, December, January, February, for a comparatively small outlay.

The climate, the soil, and atmospheric condition of Hyères facilitate the growth and cultivation of an infinite number of plants, many being of semi-tropical origin. The firm of Messrs Ch. Huber & Co. have been established for now thirty years; their gardens extend over thirty-five acres of ground covered with the finest specimens of exotic vegetation, of flowers, of evergreens, of Date Palms, Eucalyptus, Jacaranda of Brazil, Mimosa, Erythrines, the Laurels and Palms of the Canary Islands, Japanese Bamboos, Banana Trees, rare creepers, the Kennedya, etc., and various curiosities.

A CATALOGUE MAY BE OBTAINED FREE ON APPLICATION.

777.5.80

HOTEL DE L' EUROPE.

——:o:——

Occupying the most Central and the most sheltered position in the Town. There are two Large Terraces where a magnificent view can be obtained of the Sea and the Islands.

In its charges, the Hotel de l'Europe is the most moderate among the well frequented and comfortable Hotels of Hyères.

Boarders from 7 frs. to 10 frs. per day according to the room.

Good French and Provençal Cuisine, including Bouillabaisse once a week during the season, and a Sound Dinner Wine Free from extra charge.

Carriages for Excursions at the Hotel and Omnibus to meet every Train.

M. GIRAUD, Manager.   963.5.80

A. St. JOSEPH,

FIRST CLASS LINEN DRAPERS ESTABLISHMENT.

Madame Vve. LOUIT,

Purveyors to Her Majesty the Queen of Spain.

——:o:——

English Flannels and other Foreign Goods, Silk, Linen, Mourning Attire, Carpets, Bed and Bedding, Downs and Feathers.

PATENT MOSQUITO CURTAINS, HONOURABLE MENTION.

These Mosquito Curtains will suit every sort of Bed without any Iron Frame, and are therefore infinitely preferable to any other contrivance. As Ornaments they are sufficiently elegant to be used instead of Bed Curtains. They are made of strong tulle and easily washed : and can be rolled up in a trunk for travelling and weigh only 2½lbs.

SIZE AND PRICE.

No. 1, Height	. . .	2m 50	Width	. . .	7m	. . .	28 fr.
No. 2,	— . . .	2m 80	—	. . .	8m	. . .	35 ,,
No. 3,	— . . .	3m ,,	—	. . .	9m	. . .	40 ,,
No. 4,	— . . .	3m 25	—	. . .	10m	. . .	45 ,,

Hyères.—35, Rue Massillon.
PARIS DEPOT.—Maison Foye Davenne.
26, Avenue de l'Opéra,   874.5 80

E. AURENGE DECAMP,

LATE PATTESON,

CELEBRATED OLD ESTABLISHED ENGLISH HOUSE,

Grocers, Butchers, & Pork Butchers.

All English Goods kept in stock including Huntley and Palmer's Biscuits, Crosse and Blackwell's Pickles, &c. Dundee Marmalades, Colman's Mustard, York Hams, Bacon, Alsopp and Bass' Ales, Australian Tinned Meats and Soups, Price's Night Lights, Scotch Oatmeal, Brand's Essence of Meat, Cocoatina, &c., &c.
Excellent Salad and Lamp Oils, Marseilles Soap, Italian Maccaroni, Coffees, Teas, and French Groceries.

WINES AND LIQUEURS,

4, RUE PORTALET, 4.

865.5.80

BOULANGERIE DES PALMIERS.

English Bakers,

PLACE DES PALMIERS

English Bread, English Buns,
and Hot Cross Buns, Brown Bread and various Fancy Breads.
Viennese and Russian Bread, Milk, Rye, and other Bread.
Superior Croissants, Brioches, Fancy and home made Biscuits.

:o:

OLD ESTABLISHED HOUSE,

M. MARQUAND.

876,5,80

Hotel Du Beau Sejour,

QUARTIER LAZARINE.

FIRST CLASS ARISTOCRATIC AND HIGHLY LUXURIOUS HOTEL.

The minutest care, the most attentive service, and excellent cuisine secured.

An ambulance carriage at the station to meet invalids. Patent apparatus for inhalations within the rooms.

A Band will play frequently on the premises of the Hotel during dinner hour.

Balls and Concerts will be constantly given at the Hotel free from all charge to Visitors and Residents.

Picnics, Excursions, &c., will be organised at the Hotel, and every form of amusement and distraction provided free.

A Reading Room with Forty French and Foreign Newspapers.

BILLIARD ROOMS, DRAWING ROOMS, &c.

Parquet floors to every room and careful ventilation of the entire building.

Proprietor, GUEIT MAUREL.

873.5.80

Liquor of the Fenouillet.

Messrs. CABRAN & Co.,

DISTILLERS AND MERCHANTS

LA CRAU HYÈRES (VAR).

(Reward at the Paris Universal Exibition of 1878, and at the
Exhibition of Arts applied to Industry of 1879.)

This Liquor is made with the herbs which grow on the
rich and verdant mountain of the Fenouillet.   Even in the
time of the ancient Romans these herbs were renowned for
the delicacy of their flavour; the mountain deriving its
name from fæniculum, the Latin for fine herbs.

The Liquor has found high favour at all the winter
stations, Hyères, Cannes, Nice, &c., it possesses all the
digestive and hygienic qualities of Chartreuse to which it
is preferred by an ever increasing number of real
connoisseurs.

Ladies have more especially recognized its superior
merits; and all the most distinguished foreigners who have
visited the Riviera have tasted, approved and largely
employed this most agreeable and wholesome Liquor.

Depots of the Fenouillet Liquor will be found in all
the Wines Shops, Cafés, and similar Establishments.

The Liquor is exported to several foreign countries.

870.5.80

POULTERER & PROVISION MERCHANT

M. MOURÉ,

ROUTE NATIONALE AND PLACE PORTALET.

ESTABLISHED IN 1830.

Poultry from Toulouse and La Bresse, Wild Ducks and other Game, Pâté de Foie Gras, English Specialities, Guiness' Stout, Geo. Roe & Co.'s Dublin Whiskey, English Jams, Calf's Foot Jelly, Pickles, Tinned Australian and English Meats, English Biscuits, &c.

ENGLISH SPOKEN.   878.5.80

GROCERS & PROVISION MERCHANTS.

L. RIMBAUD,

10, RUE MASSILLON 10.

Fresh and preserved fruits, Smoked tongues, Strasbourg Sauerkraut, Sausages, York hams, *Foie gras*, English groceries and preserves; Poultry from Toulouse and La Bresse, Game, &c., &c.   877.5.80

English and French Pastry Cooks.

L^NT· ROUARD,

Route Nationale at the corner of the Avenue de la Gare.

Plum cakes, mince pies, hot cakes, English biscuits and all description of English pastry to order. French pastry, bonbons, game pies, Pâté de Foie gras, ices and preserved fruits, LIQUEURS AND SYRUPS.   872.5.80

ENGLISH BAKER.
M. OLLIVIER,
8, RUE MASSILLON.

English bread, Fancy bread, Vienna bread, excellent *croissants*, English and French biscuits, Pastes and Maccaronies of Italy and Naples.

BREAD ETC., DELIVERED REGULARLY AT THE HOUSE.

883.5.80

BUTCHERS.

M. BOERI,
19, Rue, Liman.

(Behind the Porte Fenouillet.)

English joints cut. Meat free from fat specially cut to make beef tea for invalids. No meat not of the first quality sold.

HIGHLY RECOMMENDED BY ENGLISH RESIDENTS.

882.5.80

Madame V^{VE} GUIRAND,

PLACE DES PALMIERS,

OLD ESTABLISHED HOUSE,
HIGHLY RECOMMENDED BY THE ENGLISH COLONY.

....

SCOTCH WHISKY specially imported direct from Inverness. IRISH WHISKYS, GINS, ALLSOPP'S ALES, Etc., Etc. All French and Local Wines and Champagnes.   881.5.80

JULES ARNAUD,
Place de Strasbourg, à Hyères (Var)
EVERY DESCRIPTION OF CARRIAGES.
Price of Excursions.

	FRS.				FRS.
1 HORSE,	7	Par	Costebelle, retour par l'Almanarre.	2 HORSES,	12
,,	7	,,	Carqueiranne, retour par la Moutonne.	,,	12
,,	12	,,	Carqueiraune à Toulon, retour par La Vallette.	,,	25
,,		,,	Giens, retour par la Pinette.	,,	20
,,	8	,,	La Castille, retour par la Chapelle et la Pauline.	,,	15
,,	8	,,	Vallée de Sauvebonne, retour par Gapeau.	,,	12
,,		,,	Les Vieux-Salins et Bormettes.—Brégançon.	,,	25

Journeys to Saint-Tropez, Cannes and Nice.—Omnibuses for Pic-nics.

872.5.80

HYÈRES
HOTEL DES ETRANGERS.

This hotel, considerably enlarged, commands a full view of the Mediterranean and the Islands of Hyères. The Southern aspect, the proximity of the Boulevard des Palmiers, the English and French Churches, the excellent table, the moderate terms and thorough comfort of the hotel, have ensured the patronage of numerous families and many distinguished visitors.

ENGLISH SPOKEN.
THE HOTEL OMNIBUS TO EVERY TRAIN.

841.5.80

ALLEVARD-LES-BAINS.
HOTEL DU LOUVRE ET DE LA PLATA.

On leaving Hyères, visitors and invalids will find at Allevard-les-Bains an excellent intermediary station. From the above hotel an admirable view is obtained of the glaciers and the mountains. The hotel is surrounded by shady walks. There is a large drawing room, a billiard room, and horses and carriages for excursions. Many families frequent this summer residence where they find every comfort, elegant apartments, a good table and wine for a moderate charge.

OMNIBUS TO THE STATION OF GONCELIN ALLEVARD.
Proprietor and Director of both the above Establishments,

F. BERTHET.

841.5.80

French and English Library.

---o---

MADAME TROTOBAT,

Place des Palmiers.

---o---

Circulating library of English and French novels
and various standard works, in all about 5000 volumes.

Extensive assortment of stationery, of all the necessary
articles for painting and drawing, Christmas books, picture
books for children, Christmas cards, &c., &c.

WELL KNOWN AND HIGHLY RECOMMENDED
OLD ESTABLISHED HOUSE.

866.5.80

CAFÉ DE L'UNIVERS,

AVENUE DE LA GARE,

M. OUTRON (Proprietor).

---o---

REFRESHMENTS OF THE PUREST
DESCRIPTION AND OF THE BEST BRANDS.

Strasbourg and English Ales.

All the light beverages suited to the Southern
Climate are provided at this ESTABLISHMENT.

ENGLISH NEWSPAPERS.

880.5.80

THE ENGLISH BANK,
HYÈRES.

The Bank is in correspondence with all the leading English, Scotch, and American Banks, and cashes their Circular Notes and Drafts, and makes payments on letters of credit. Special and favourable terms are allowed to clients keeping deposit accounts.

To ensure comfortable and healthy Villas and Apartments a Register of all that can be recommended is kept by the (English) House Agent appointed by the Bank. All letters should be addressed "THE ENGLISH HOUSE AGENT, care of THE ENGLISH BANK, HYÈRES," and stamps (English or French) enclosed for reply. Two large Villas belonging to the Bank, the sanitary arrangements of which have been carried out in accordance with the latest improvements, and pronounced perfect by high medical authority are on this Register.

The London correspondents of the Agency, Messrs. Flageollet, Lombard Street, will receive and forward luggage to Hyères, where it can be stored for any period, together with supplies of all kinds which can be obtained through the Agency in London at prices not higher than the co-operative stores.

Arrangements have been made with some of the leading Vineyard Proprietors in Bordeaux, Burgundy, and Epernay to deliver the best red and white Wines and Champagne in London at growers' prices.

This Agency undertakes the Sale and Purchase of Land and Houses.   818.5.80

GRAND HOTEL DU PARC

HYÈRES (VAR).

A. WATTEBLED DE LYON,

PROPRIETAIRE.

SITUATED in the centre of the Avenue of Palms. Formerly the Chateau Fanoux which was inhabited by Queen Christine of Sweden. Surrounded by a fine garden where some of the best specimens of the exotic vegetation of Hyères may be seen: the Date Palms and Canary Palms, Myrtle, Aloes, Cactus, etc.

THE 'TIMES' AND OTHER ENGLISH PAPERS.

Reading and Smoking Rooms, etc.

THE WATER COMPANY'S PURE SUPPLY LAID ON.

THE MOST SHELTERED POSITION.   SPLENDID VIEW.

OMNIBUS TO EVERY TRAIN.

840.5.80

HOTEL DES AMBASSADEURS,

AUGUSTE SUZANNE, Proprietor.

FIRST CLASS, ESTABLISHMENT NEWLY REBUILT AND FURNISHED.

Well sheltered and Windows to the full South commanding a magnificent view of the Mediterranean and the Islands of Hyères.

The Hotel is in the centre of the town, at the foot of the Chateau Hill on the Route Nationale between the Place des Palmiers and the Avenue des Palmiers, and is therefore one of the warmest and best sheltered hotels of Hyères.

The Company's water laid on to every floor ; the drains have been newly repaired and carefully ventilated by a special shaft, and the utmost cleanliness is observed.

All the linen is taken and washed at a private farm belonging to the Hotel and situated at some distance from the town where there is an abundant running and pure stream. The linen is thus kept apart, and the danger of contamination obviated.

From this Farm, Eggs that are really fresh and other Provisions are obtained.

GOOD FRENCH AND ENGLISH CUISINE.

OMNIBUS AT THE STATION
AND CARRIAGES FOR EXCURSIONS, &c.

863.5.80

GRAND HOTEL D'ORIENT.

THIS HOTEL is situated in the most salubrious and sheltered part of Hyères, and is the resort of the élite of French and English Society.

Comfortable and Airy Rooms.

THE HOTEL IS SUPPLIED WITH THE PUREST WATER BY

THE TOWN WATER COMPANY.

English Newspapers, 'Times', &c.

SMOKING ROOM, DRAWING ROOMS, &c.

OMNIBUS TO EVERY TRAIN.

Proprietor, CH. CAUVIN.

PREPAID SCALE OF CHARGES

In the 'Carnarvon and Denbigh Herald,' 'Herald Cymraeg' and 'Llandudno Register.'

Lost, Found, &c. Wanted Servants. Wanted Clerks, Assistants. Wanted Workme
Wanted Apprentices and Boys. Wanted Houses, &c. Wanted Misce laneous. T
be let Apartments. To be let Houses, Land, &c. To be let Sale-shops, &c. To b
let Workshops, &c. To be let Public-Houses. To be sold Houses, Land. To b
sold Machinery, &c.

All short Advertisements may be inserted as below.

The above may be advertised at the following exceptionally Lov
Rates, if prepaid by Post Office Orders. No receipts are sent, the
appearance of the Advertisement being the acknowledgment If replie
to Advertisements are made to the 'HERALD' Office, an additional sixpence
must be sent with order to cover postage of replies to Advertisements
which are posted on Tuesday and Saturday weekly.

WORDS.	ONE INSERTION.		THREE INSERTIONS.		SIX INSERTIONS.	
	In either Herald.	C. & D. Herald and Herald Cymraeg.	In either Herald.	C. & D. Herald and Herald Cymraeg.	In either Herald.	C. & D. Herald and Herald Cymraeg.
	s. d.	s. d.	s. d.	s. d.	s. d.	s. d.
18	1 6	2 6	3 0	4 6	4 6	7 6
27	2 0	3 0	3 6	5 9	5 9	9 0
36	2 6	3 6	4 0	6 6	6 0	9 6
45	3 0	4 6	4 6	7 6	6 9	10 6
54	3 6	5 0	5 0	8 0	7 6	12 6
63	4 0	6 0	5 6	9 6	8 6	14 6

The rates are strictly confined to the class of Advertisements enumer-
ated above, AND MUST BE PREPAID, by remittance in Half-penny Stamps
in Registered letter, or by Post Office Order, payable to JOHN EVANS
& COMPANY, 'Herald' Office, Carnarvon.

NOTE.—Sixpence extra to be sent if replies are made to the office to
cover postage to advertise.

Otherwise they will be charged Credit scale.

Notices of Births, Deaths, and Marriages, are charged 2s. 6d. each,
including copy of the paper. In all cases they must be authenticated by
the name and address of the sender.

☞ *Advertisements received and inserted in all London, Liverpool,
Manchester, &c., newspapers, at the same price as if
sent direct.*

In force until 31st December, 1881.

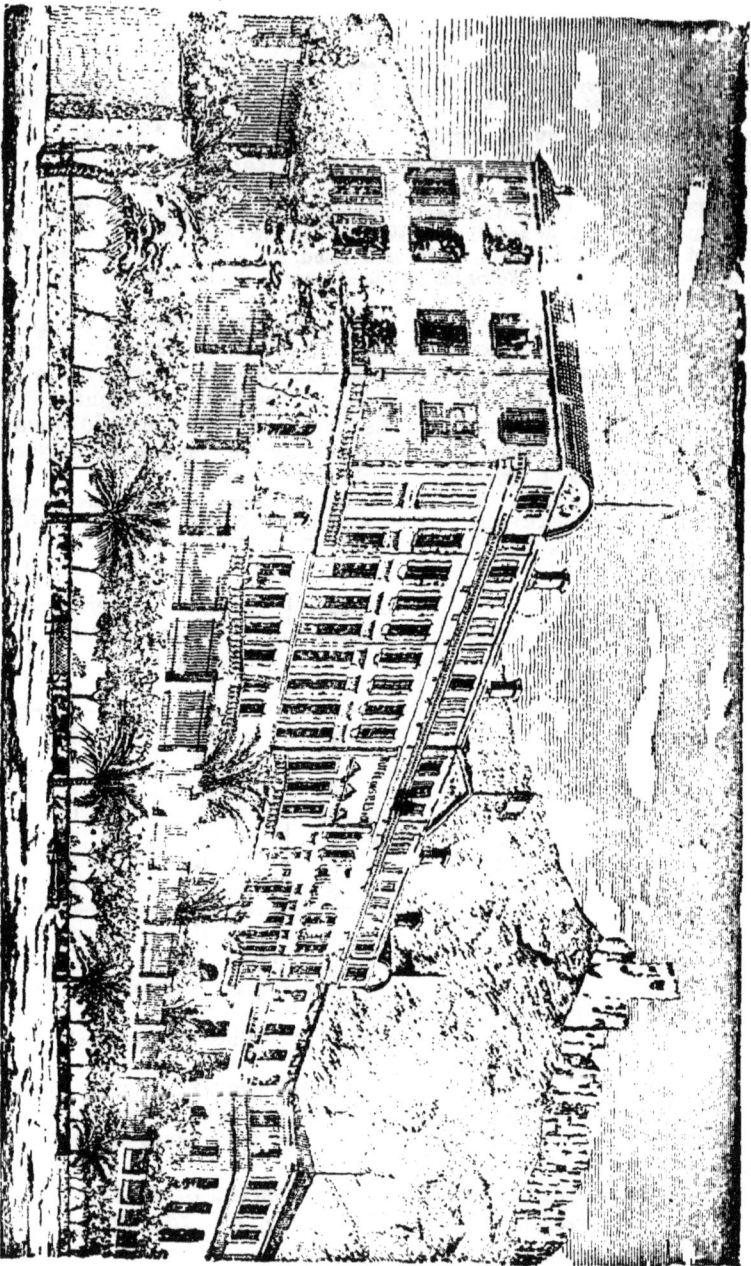

E. WEBER

GRAND HÔTEL DES ÎLES D'OR A HYÈRES (VAR)

www.ingramcontent.com/pod-product-compliance
Lightning Source LLC
Chambersburg PA
CBHW050007100426
42739CB00011B/2542